Stir-Fry

GENERAL EDITOR
Chuck Williams

RECIPES
Diane Rossen Worthington

PHOTOGRAPHY
Allan Rosenberg

TIME
LIFE
BOOKS

Time-Life Books is a division of
TIME LIFE INCORPORATED

President and CEO: John M. Fahey, Jr.
President, Time-Life Books: John D. Hall

TIME-LIFE CUSTOM PUBLISHING

Vice President and Publisher: Terry Newell
Sales Director: Frances C. Mangan
Editorial Director: Robert A. Doyle

WILLIAMS-SONOMA
Founder/Vice-Chairman: Chuck Williams

WELDON OWEN INC.
President: John Owen
Publisher: Wendely Harvey
Managing Editor: Laurie Wertz
Consulting Editor: Norman Kolpas
Copy Editor: Sharon Silva
Editorial Assistant: Janique Poncelet
Design: John Bull, The Book Design Company
Production: James Obata, Stephanie Sherman,
   Mick Bagnato
Food Photographer: Allan Rosenberg
Additional Food Photography: Allen V. Lott
Primary Food & Prop Stylist: Sandra Griswold
Food Stylist: Heidi Gintner
Assistant Food Stylist: Mara Barot
Glossary Illustrations: Alice Harth

The Williams-Sonoma Kitchen Library
conceived and produced by Weldon Owen Inc.
814 Montgomery St., San Francisco, CA 94133

In collaboration with Williams-Sonoma
100 North Point, San Francisco, CA 94133

Production by Mandarin Offset, Hong Kong
Printed in China

A Note on Weights and Measures:
All recipes include customary U.S. and metric
measurements. Metric conversions are based on
a standard developed for these books and have
been rounded off. Actual weights may vary.

A Weldon Owen Production

Copyright © 1994 Weldon Owen Inc.
All rights reserved, including the right of
reproduction in whole or in part in any form.

Library of Congress
Cataloging-in-Publication Data:

Worthington, Diane Rossen.
    Stir-fry / recipes, Diane Rossen Worthington ;
photography, Allan Rosenberg.
        p.   cm. — (Williams-Sonoma kitchen library)
    Includes index.
    ISBN 0-7835-0300-8
    1. Stir frying.   2. Wok cookery.   3. Skillet cookery.
I. Title.   II. Series.
TX689.5.W67   1994
641.7'7—dc20   93-49010
                                                          CIP

Contents

MEAT & POULTRY 15

SEAFOOD 45

RICE & NOODLES 63

VEGETABLES 81

INTRODUCTION

I remember a time not long ago when the stir-frying craze first swept from Asia to the West. Every cookware store offered boxed wok kits containing the familiar Chinese rounded pan, a lid and assorted stirring tools. Everyone, it seemed, was slicing and stirring like mad.

Like most fads, that one passed—and a lot of those old woks are gathering dust and rust on hard-to-reach shelves. That's a shame, because stir-frying is not only easy but also healthful, using minimal fats and preserving the nutritive value of ingredients through quick cooking. At the same time, however, the decline of stir-frying justly reflected the fact that many cooks soon felt limited by meal after meal of bite-sized foods seasoned primarily with soy sauce.

This book aims to restore stir-frying to the position of importance it justly deserves, broadening its appeal with recipes that find their inspiration in Europe and the Americas as well as in Asia. You'll find many recipes featuring non-Asian ingredients and seasonings from Italian, French, Mexican and other cuisines of the Western world. You'll also find side dishes you can quickly stir-fry and serve with any main course of your choosing.

The book begins with a discussion of the kitchen equipment you'll need, along with step-by-step photographic guidelines to basic stir-frying techniques. The 45 recipes that follow are divided into chapters by their featured ingredients. More than anything else, I wanted to make these recipes accessible to as many cooks as possible. To that end, you'll find that many use seasonings and garnishes that do not require a trip to an ethnic market. And all of the recipes can be made with a traditional wok or with an ordinary frying pan or sauté pan.

I'm sure you'll be surprised by what a valuable addition stir-frying can make to your culinary repertoire.

Chuck Williams

EQUIPMENT

Familiar and foreign tools for the simple art of stir-frying

Stir-frying calls for only a few basic pieces of equipment—most of which can already be found in any home kitchen. Good-quality knives, for example, are essential for cutting up food into small, uniform pieces that will cook quickly and evenly. A set of mixing bowls in various sizes is useful for holding ingredients close at hand, ready to be added at the right moment in the cooking sequence.

While not absolutely essential, some Asian utensils and cookware will make stir-frying easier. Pre-eminent among these is a wok, the Chinese pan whose hemispherical shape provides an ideal cooking surface for stir-frying. Those shown here include adaptations for the contemporary Western kitchen. Made of stainless or enameled steel instead of the traditional milled steel, they require no seasoning with hot oil or other special care to maintain their surfaces; and their flat bottoms, in place of the traditional rounded bottoms, rest solidly atop electric and gas stove tops alike.

1. Stockpot
Tall, deep, large-capacity pot with close-fitting lid, for making stock or for cooking noodles or pasta. Strainer insert allows noodles to be drained or stock ingredients to be removed easily after cooking. Select a good-quality, heavy pot that absorbs and transfers heat well, such as the enameled metal shown here.

2. Assorted Utensils
Crockery jar holds a variety of utensils for use in stir-frying: long-handled wok spatula and wooden spoon for stirring ingredients during cooking; ladle for transferring and serving liquid mixtures; wooden forks for tossing and serving noodles and fluffing rice; whisk for stirring sauce and seasoning mixtures; wooden tongs for turning large ingredients and for tossing noodles.

3. Cutting Board
Acrylic boards are tough, resilient, nonporous and easy to clean. Be sure to wash thoroughly after every use.

4. Mixing Bowls

Sturdy bowls in a wide range of sizes for holding cut-up ingredients, seasonings and sauces before or during cooking, or for marinating meats, poultry or seafood.

5. Zester

Small, sharp holes at end of stainless-steel blade cut citrus zest into fine shreds.

6. Paring Knife and Chef's Knife

The small paring knife trims and peels vegetables and cuts up small ingredients. The larger chef's knife chops and slices large items or large quantities of ingredients.

7. Chinese Cleaver

Traditional shaped cleaver has heavy blade with curved edge for easy chopping and slicing of ingredients. Choose a sturdy, well-balanced model with a sharp, stainless-steel blade attached to a sturdy handle that feels comfortable in the hand.

8. Colander and Strainer

For washing and draining rice and stir-fry ingredients and for straining stock and oil. Choose stainless steel; enameled-steel colanders are also good choices.

9. Saucepan

For parboiling or otherwise precooking ingredients before they are stir-fried, and for cooking rice. Select a good-quality, heavy pot that absorbs and transfers heat well. Enameled metal, shown here, cleans easily and does not react with acidic ingredients such as wine, citrus juice or tomatoes.

10. Small Wok

For use when stir-frying small quantities. Flat bottom makes the wok adaptable to gas or electric stoves.

11. Kitchen Chopsticks

Extra-long, heavy-duty wooden chopsticks for stirring and turning ingredients during cooking.

12. Wire Skimmer

Long-handled skimmer with wide bowl and fine mesh efficiently and safely lifts and drains deep-fried foods being fried in a wok. Also removes froth and scum from surface of stock during its preparation.

13. Wok

Traditionally shaped half-spherical pan for easy stir-frying. Choose a heavy stainless-steel, aluminum, or traditional milled steel wok that conducts heat evenly and holds it well. Tight-fitting lid allows foods to steam-cook until done. Contemporary flat-bottomed design allows the wok to be used with equal ease on electric or gas stoves.

14. Frying Pan

A large, wide frying pan with sloping sides may be used in place of a wok for stir-frying. A straight-sided sauté pan is also a good choice. Choose good-quality, heavy stainless steel, thick aluminum or heavy enamel, all of which conduct and hold heat well.

15. Measuring Cups and Spoons

In graduated sizes, for measuring larger and smaller quantities of ingredients.

STIR-FRY BASICS

Simple, logical steps for an age-old cooking technique

Although stir-frying, a classic technique of the Chinese kitchen, may understandably seem foreign to some cooks, it holds no great mystery. Every aspect of stir-frying, in fact, stems logically from a quest for simplicity and economy.

Fuel for cooking has historically been scarce in China, particularly in the south where stir-frying first developed. Precious wood was heated in small, narrow earthenware stoves with circular openings. The *wok*—Cantonese for "pot"—rested neatly on such an opening and, made of heavy steel shaped into a hemisphere, conducted and held heat efficiently. Every step of the stir-frying process, in turn, proceeds with similar efficiency.

The first step is preparation. All ingredients are cut into uniform, relatively small pieces that will cook quickly and evenly (see examples, below); strips or chunks of meat, poultry or seafood that require marinating are mixed with their seasonings. Then, every element of the stir-fry recipe, down to the smallest measures of liquids, oils and seasonings, are conveniently arranged so they are close at hand during cooking.

High heat ensures that foods cook quickly. To that end, the wok or frying pan is first placed over high heat on the stove top and heated until a drop of water dances and then evaporates immediately on contact. Then, the required amount of oil is drizzled in around the sides of the pan, heating as it is swirled to coat the interior and flow to the center. The oil's heat may be tested with a single piece of the first ingredient to be added, which should sizzle briskly on contact.

CUTTING TECHNIQUES

Cutting into chunks.
To cut meat into chunks, trim it—here, boneless skinless chicken breasts—of any fat or membranes. Using a sharp knife, cut into thick strips, then cut each strip crosswise into even chunks.

Cutting into strips.
Vegetables cook quickly and evenly when cut into thin strips. Using a sharp knife, cut vegetables into sections of uniform length. Cut each section in half lengthwise. Steadying each piece cut side down, slice it lengthwise into strips of uniform thickness.

Cutting into diagonal slices.
Cylindrical vegetables such as asparagus, green (spring) onions and carrots are often sliced on the diagonal—that is, at an angle—which allows them to cook more quickly because more interior surface is exposed.

Ingredients are then added in a logical order. Flavorings such as garlic and ginger, which season the oil to the point where they give off a pronounced aroma, may be added first. Next, meat may be added, or dense vegetables such as carrots, followed in order by those ingredients that require progressively less cooking time. The actual order will vary with specific recipes and how particular ingredients are prepared, but the desired result remains constant: a mixture of ingredients each of which is perfectly cooked, with the meat, poultry or seafood lightly seared, tender and succulent, and the vegetables tender-crisp and vibrantly colored.

Toward the end of cooking, liquids and seasonings are usually added; the pan may be covered with a lid at this stage and the heat reduced, if the mixture requires steaming to complete the cooking. Finally, cornstarch dissolved in a little liquid may be added to thicken the sauce and lightly glaze the ingredients.

1. Marinating the main ingredient.
In a mixing bowl, stir together all the marinade ingredients. Add the main ingredient—here, pieces of chicken breast—and turn to coat evenly. Leave at room temperature, or covered in the refrigerator, for the time specified in the recipe.

2. Beginning to stir-fry.
Heat a wok or large frying pan over high heat. Pour in oil around the sides. When the oil is hot, add aromatic vegetables or any hard, dense vegetables such as carrots that need longer cooking time.

3. Cooking the vegetables.
Stir and toss the vegetables vigorously with a long spatula. When the longer-cooking vegetables are almost done, add those that cook more quickly, such as mushrooms, corn and snow peas. Continue stirring and tossing until almost tender-crisp.

4. Cooking the main ingredient.
Remove the vegetable mixture from the pan and set aside. Add a little more oil to the pan and heat it. Add the chicken, then stir and toss until it loses any trace of pink color. Be sure to spread the meat in the pan so that it cooks evenly.

5. Adding the sauce.
Return all the vegetables to the pan. Quickly stir the sauce and add it to the pan. Bring to a boil and stir and toss until the sauce lightly coats the ingredients.

6. Serving the stir-fry.
Transfer the contents of the pan to a warmed serving bowl or platter. Use a spoon, fork or pair of chopsticks to quickly rearrange some of the ingredients for the most attractive presentation. Serve immediately.

FRIED RICE

A classic Chinese way to make good use of leftovers

Although its name may imply otherwise, fried rice is actually *stir-fried* rice. The preparation evolved as a convenient way for Chinese cooks to use up leftover rice, quickly stir-frying it with other bits of meat and vegetable to make a casual side dish or main course.

The procedure for making fried rice may vary from recipe to recipe, but the principles remain the same, beginning with the rice itself. Long-grain rice, the standard in China, makes the best choice. If you have no leftover rice, you must cook rice far enough in advance to allow time for it to cool completely in the refrigerator, so its grains can be easily separated by hand.

Next, scrambled egg—a typical garnish—is usually cooked in the pan and removed. Following that, the additional ingredients are stir-fried and then tossed together with the rice and seasoned before finally mixing with the egg.

Salt is the traditional Chinese seasoning for fried rice, as it preserves the white rice's pristine color; soy sauce is another popular choice. But extending the concept of fried rice beyond its Asian borders opens up a wide range of possibilities for flavoring and embellishing this versatile preparation.

1. Separating the rice.
If there is not enough leftover rice, precook rice following the instructions on page 12. Let cool, then refrigerate until cold. With wet fingers, gently rub the rice to separate clumps into individual grains.

2. Cooking the egg.
Heat a wok or large frying pan over medium heat. Pour in oil around the sides. When the oil is hot, add beaten egg and gently stir until it forms soft curds. Transfer the egg to a bowl and set aside.

3. Stir-frying the rice.
Heat more oil and stir-fry the other ingredients until the meat is done or heated through and the vegetables are tender-crisp. Add the rice and stir-fry until heated through. Season to taste. Add the egg and stir to break it into small, evenly distributed pieces.

Three-Color Fried Rice

Stir-Frying Noodles

A quick toss in the wok for a wide variety of Asian noodles

All manner of Asian noodles—from rice sticks to mung bean threads to robust wheat-and-egg mein—may be stir-fried with meat, poultry, seafood, eggs, liquids and seasonings to make satisfying side dishes or main courses.

Because most noodles are relatively delicate, their time in the wok or frying pan is short—only long enough to toss well and absorb some of the sauce after the other ingredients have been stir-fried.

1. Preparing the noodles.
Before stir-frying commences, precook or otherwise prepare the noodles. In this case, rice sticks—which are manufactured from already-cooked rice—are soaked in water to soften, and then thoroughly drained.

2. Stir-frying the noodles.
Stir and toss the other ingredients—in this case, a mixture of shrimp and egg. After the liquid seasonings are added, stir in the noodles thoroughly so they evenly absorb the sauce. Here, bean sprouts have been tossed in after the noodles, to add a crisp note.

Thai Noodles

Toasting Nuts

Toasted nuts add flavor and crunch to many stir-fries. Nuts—here, slivered blanched almonds—are easily toasted by stirring and tossing in a dry wok or pan over medium heat until they turn an even golden brown. Take care not to over-toast; the nuts will continue to darken after they're removed from the pan.

Steamed White Rice

This simply cooked rice is the traditional accompaniment for stir-fries. Its mild taste and whiteness contrast well with the more definite flavors and brighter colors of most stir-fry dishes. Left to cool, the steamed rice can also be used for making fried rice.

1 cup (7 oz/220 g) long-grain white rice
1½ cups (12 fl oz/375 ml) water

Place the rice in a colander and rinse with cold water to remove excess starch. Drain well.

Combine the rice and the water in a saucepan over medium-high heat. Bring to a boil and boil, uncovered, until most of the water evaporates and there are crater-like holes in the surface of the rice, about 10 minutes.

Reduce the heat to low, cover tightly and simmer until the rice is tender, 10–15 minutes longer. Remove from the heat and let stand, covered, for about 10 minutes before serving.

Just before serving, fluff the rice with a fork, then serve immediately.

Makes about 3 cups (15 oz/470 g); serves 4–6

All-Purpose Stir-Fry Sauce

Here is a great sauce to have around for last-minute stir-fry dishes. It works with any meat, seafood or vegetables. Simply add it near the end of cooking. This amount is sufficient to season about 1 pound (500 g) of ingredients, but you can make the sauce in whatever quantity you like; it will keep in a jar with a tight-fitting lid for up to 1 week in the refrigerator. If you do make it in advance, add the green onion just before using.

3 tablespoons soy sauce
1 teaspoon finely chopped, peeled fresh ginger
1 small clove garlic, minced
1 green (spring) onion, including tender green tops, finely chopped
½ teaspoon chili oil *(recipe on page 13)*

In a small bowl, combine the soy sauce, ginger, garlic, green onion and chili oil and stir well.

Makes about ¼ cup (2 fl oz/60 ml)

Chili Oil

Use this both as a seasoning for cooking and as a table condiment. During its preparation, do not lean directly over the pan as the oil heats, because the chili peppers release very pungent fumes that may irritate your eyes. If you like, leave the pepper flakes in the oil; they will make it hotter the longer it stands. The oil keeps indefinitely in a small glass jar with a tight-fitting lid in the refrigerator.

4 tablespoons red pepper flakes
1 cup (8 fl oz/250 ml) peanut, canola or safflower oil

*I*n a small saucepan over medium heat, combine the pepper flakes and oil. Bring almost to a boil, then turn off the heat and let cool. Strain into a glass container with a lid.

Makes 1 cup (8 fl oz/250 ml)

Chinese-Style Chicken Stock

Use this aromatic stock when you need a chicken stock with an Asian accent. For convenience, it can be frozen in small containers for up to 2 months, and then reboiled before using.

2 lb (1 kg) chicken necks and backs
1 celery stalk, cut into ½-inch (12-mm) lengths
2 small carrots, peeled and cut into ½-inch (12-mm) lengths
1 yellow onion, cut in half
1 leek, including tender green tops, carefully washed and sliced
2 green (spring) onions, including tender green tops, cut into 2-inch (5-cm) lengths
2 slices fresh ginger, each ⅛ inch (3 mm) thick, peeled
salt and pepper

*C*ombine the chicken pieces, celery, carrots, yellow onion, leek, green onions, ginger and salt and pepper to taste in a 4-qt (4-l) saucepan. Add enough cold water to fill the pan three-fourths full. Place over medium heat, uncovered, and bring slowly to a boil. Skim off any scum that forms on the surface. Reduce the heat to its lowest possible setting and simmer, uncovered, for 2½ hours. Skim the scum off the surface as needed.
Strain through a sieve or colander lined with cheesecloth (muslin) into a storage container. Taste and adjust the seasonings. Let cool, then cover and refrigerate. Using a large spoon, lift off the fat that solidifies on the surface and discard. If not using the stock immediately, pour into 1 or more containers, cover tightly and refrigerate for up to 3 days.

Makes about 6 cups (48 fl oz/1.5 l)

Chicken with Plum Sauce

1½ lb (750 g) boneless, skinless
   chicken breasts, cut into 1½-inch
   (4-cm) chunks
1 tablespoon cornstarch
1 tablespoon dry sherry
1 tablespoon soy sauce
2 teaspoons natural rice vinegar
2 tablespoons peanut or vegetable oil
¾ cup (3 oz/90 g) canned water
   chestnuts, rinsed, well drained
   and halved
6 green (spring) onions, including
   tender green tops, cut into 2-inch
   (5-cm) lengths and then sliced
   lengthwise
3 tablespoons plum sauce
½ cup (4 fl oz/125 ml) Chinese-style
   chicken stock *(recipe on page 13)*

*Crisp, mild water chestnuts are a good counterpoint to the
sweet yet pungent plum sauce in this flavorful dish. You can
find plum sauce, which is used as both an ingredient and as a
dipping sauce in Chinese cuisine, in Asian markets and well-
stocked food stores.*

*P*lace the chicken pieces in a bowl and sprinkle with the
cornstarch. Toss to coat and add the sherry, soy sauce and
vinegar, tossing again to coat evenly.

In a wok or frying pan over high heat, warm the oil,
swirling to coat the bottom and sides of the pan. When
the oil is very hot but not quite smoking, add the chicken
pieces and stir and toss every 15–20 seconds until opaque
and firm, 5–6 minutes. Using a slotted spoon, transfer to
a dish.

Add the water chestnuts and green onions to the oil
remaining in the pan and stir and toss every 15–20 seconds
until the onions are just wilted, 1–2 minutes. Add the
plum sauce and chicken stock and bring to a boil. Return
the chicken pieces to the pan and heat through, about
1 minute.

Taste and adjust the seasonings. Serve immediately.

Serves 4–6

Beef with Orange-Chili Sauce

FOR THE SAUCE:

⅓ cup (3 fl oz/80 ml) chicken stock, preferably Chinese style (*recipe on page 13*)

2 tablespoons soy sauce

finely grated zest of 1 orange

2 teaspoons cornstarch

4 tablespoons (2 fl oz/60 ml) peanut or vegetable oil

12 small dried red chili peppers

1 carrot, peeled and cut into thin strips 2 inches (5 cm) long and ½ inch (12 mm) wide

½ small red bell pepper (capsicum), seeded, deribbed and cut into strips 2 inches (5 cm) long and ½ inch (12 mm) wide

1 lb (500 g) flank steak, sliced in half horizontally and then cut into thin strips 2 inches (5 cm) long and ¾ inch (2 cm) wide

1 orange, peeled, with all white pith removed, then divided into segments and each segment cut in half crosswise

3 green (spring) onions, including tender green tops, thinly sliced

Warn your guests not to eat the chilies, as they are very hot. Serve with steamed white rice (page 12) or vegetable fried rice (page 63).

To make the sauce, combine the chicken stock, soy sauce, orange zest and cornstarch in a small bowl and stir to dissolve the cornstarch. Set aside.

In a wok or frying pan over medium-high heat, warm 1 tablespoon of the oil. When the oil is hot, add the chilies and stir and toss until they turn dark red, about 1 minute. Watch carefully so they do not burn. Transfer to a bowl and set aside.

Raise the heat to high and add another 1 tablespoon oil to the pan, swirling to coat the bottom and sides. When the oil is very hot but not quite smoking, add the carrot and bell pepper and stir and toss every 15–20 seconds until they begin to soften, about 2 minutes. Add to the bowl holding the chilies.

Add another 1 tablespoon oil to the pan, again swirling to coat. When very hot but not quite smoking, add half of the beef strips and stir and toss every 15–20 seconds until browned but still slightly pink inside, 2–3 minutes. Be sure to distribute the meat evenly in the pan so it comes into maximum contact with the heat and cooks evenly. Add to the bowl holding the vegetables. Add the remaining 1 tablespoon oil to the pan and cook the remaining meat in the same manner.

Return the chilies, vegetables and meat to the pan. Quickly stir the reserved sauce and add it to the pan. Stir and toss over medium-high heat until the sauce begins to thicken, about 2 minutes. Stir in the orange segments and green onions and serve immediately.

Serves 4

Lamb with Eggplant and Green Onions

FOR THE MARINADE:

1 egg white

2 tablespoons soy sauce

1 tablespoon cornstarch

1 lb (500 g) boneless lamb leg meat, cut into strips 2 inches (5 cm) long, ¾ inch (2 cm) wide and ½ inch (12 mm) thick

FOR THE SAUCE:

3 tablespoons natural rice vinegar

3 tablespoons hoisin sauce

2 tablespoons chili paste with garlic

1 teaspoon Asian sesame oil, or to taste

2 tablespoons chicken or beef stock or water

3–4 tablespoons (1½–2 fl oz/45–60 ml) peanut or vegetable oil

4 Asian (slender) eggplants (aubergines), unpeeled, cut into strips 2 inches (5 cm) long, ¾ inch (2 cm) wide and ½ inch (12 mm) thick

4 green (spring) onions, including tender green tops, cut on the diagonal into 1-inch (2.5-cm) pieces

Serve with steamed white rice (page 12) and a colorful vegetable.

❧❧

To make the marinade, combine the egg white, soy sauce and cornstarch in a bowl and stir to dissolve the cornstarch. Add the lamb strips and toss to coat. Cover and marinate for 15 minutes to 1 hour in the refrigerator.

To make the sauce, combine the vinegar, hoisin sauce, chili paste, sesame oil and stock or water in a small bowl and stir to mix well. Set aside.

In a wok or frying pan over high heat, warm 2 tablespoons of the peanut or vegetable oil, swirling to coat the bottom and sides of the pan. When the oil is very hot but not quite smoking, add the eggplant and stir and toss every 15–20 seconds until slightly softened, 3–4 minutes. Add the green onions and stir and toss for 1 minute longer. Transfer the vegetables to a bowl.

Add another 1 tablespoon oil to the pan over high heat, again swirling to coat the pan. When the oil is very hot but not quite smoking, add half of the lamb and stir and toss every 15–20 seconds until browned, 3–4 minutes. Be sure to distribute the lamb evenly in the pan so that it comes into maximum contact with the heat and cooks evenly. Transfer to the bowl holding the vegetables. Add the remaining 1 tablespoon oil, if needed, and cook the remaining lamb in the same manner.

Quickly stir the reserved sauce and add it to the pan over medium-high heat along with the reserved eggplant, onions and lamb. Cook, stirring to coat the ingredients evenly with the sauce, until the sauce thickens slightly, about 2 minutes longer. Serve immediately.

Serves 4

Beef with Caramelized Onions and Red Bell Pepper

For a touch of citrus, add 1 teaspoon chopped orange zest with the vinegar and sugar.

FOR THE MARINADE:

1 tablespoon dry sherry

1 tablespoon soy sauce

2 teaspoons cornstarch

1 lb (500 g) flank steak, sliced in half horizontally and then cut into thin strips 2 inches (5 cm) long and ¾ inch (2 cm) wide

3–4 tablespoons (1½–2 fl oz/45–60 ml) peanut or vegetable oil

1 large yellow onion, thinly sliced

1 red bell pepper (capsicum), seeded, deribbed and thinly sliced

2 tablespoons balsamic vinegar

1 teaspoon sugar

½ cup (4 fl oz/125 ml) beef stock

1 teaspoon cornstarch dissolved in 3 tablespoons water, optional

To make the marinade, combine the sherry, soy sauce and cornstarch in a bowl and stir well. Add the beef strips, toss to coat and marinate at room temperature for 15 minutes.

In a wok or frying pan over medium-high heat, warm 1 tablespoon of the oil, swirling to coat the bottom and sides of the pan. When the oil is hot, add half of the beef strips and stir and toss every 15–20 seconds until browned but still slightly pink inside, 2–3 minutes. Be sure to distribute the meat evenly in the pan so that it comes into maximum contact with the heat and cooks evenly. Transfer to a bowl. Add another 1 tablespoon oil to the pan, if needed, and cook the remaining beef in the same manner. Transfer the beef to the bowl.

Add the remaining 2 tablespoons oil to the pan over medium-high heat, again swirling to coat the pan. When the oil is hot, add the onion and stir and toss every 15–20 seconds until nicely softened, 5–7 minutes. Be sure to distribute the onions evenly in the pan so that they come into maximum contact with the heat and cook evenly. Add the bell pepper and stir and toss until it begins to soften, 2 minutes longer.

Add the vinegar and sugar and stir and toss until the onion begins to caramelize, about 2 minutes longer. Add the stock, bring to a boil over high heat and cook for 2 minutes. If you want a thicker sauce, add the optional cornstarch-water mixture.

Return the beef to the pan and stir and toss until heated through, about 30 seconds. Taste and adjust the seasonings. Serve immediately.

Serves 4

Chicken and Vegetable Curry

2 tablespoons peanut or vegetable oil

2 cloves garlic, minced

1 teaspoon finely chopped, peeled fresh ginger

1 red (Spanish) onion, finely chopped

1 lb (500 g) boneless, skinless chicken breasts, cut into 1½-inch (4-cm) chunks

3 tablespoons soy sauce

1–2 tablespoons curry powder or curry paste, or to taste

1 cup (8 fl oz/250 ml) water

1 cup (8 fl oz/250 ml) chicken stock, preferably Chinese style *(recipe on page 13)*

2 red potatoes, peeled and cut into ¾-inch (2-cm) cubes

2 carrots, peeled, halved lengthwise and cut into 2-inch (5-cm) lengths

This robust one-dish meal is made aromatic with the addition of curry powder. The strength and flavor of curry powders vary widely; an ethnic specialty market is a good place to find a broad selection. An Indian or Thai curry paste can be used in place of the curry powder and is often superior to most commercial curry powders. Serve with a big bowl of steamed white rice (recipe on page 12) and a cooling platter of fresh oranges for dessert.

*I*n a wok or frying pan over high heat, warm the oil, swirling to coat the bottom and sides of the pan. When the oil is very hot but not quite smoking, add the garlic, ginger and onion and stir and toss rapidly until the onion has just softened, 2–3 minutes. Add the chicken pieces and stir and toss every 15–20 seconds until the chicken is white and firm and no trace of pink remains, 4–5 minutes. Be sure to distribute the chicken evenly in the pan so it comes into maximum contact with the heat and cooks evenly. Transfer the chicken-onion mixture to a dish and set aside.

To the same pan over medium-high heat, add the soy sauce, curry powder or paste, water, stock, potatoes and carrots. Stir well and bring to a simmer. Reduce the heat to medium, cover and simmer for 12 minutes, stirring once after 6 minutes.

Uncover and return the chicken-onion mixture to the pan, stirring to mix evenly. Simmer until the vegetables are tender, 5–7 minutes longer. (The sauce will thicken during this time as well.)

Taste and adjust the seasonings. Serve immediately.

Serves 4

Turkey and Sugar Snap Peas with Orange-Mustard Sauce

Here is a particularly high-spirited dish, infused with the perfume of sweet oranges and French Dijon mustard.

FOR THE SAUCE:

½ cup (4 fl oz/125 ml) fresh orange juice

1 teaspoon finely chopped orange zest

1 tablespoon soy sauce

2 teaspoons finely chopped, peeled fresh ginger

1 clove garlic, minced

1 shallot, finely chopped

2 teaspoons honey

1 teaspoon Dijon mustard

FOR THE MARINADE:

1 egg white

1 tablespoon mirin or sake

2 teaspoons soy sauce

1 tablespoon cornstarch

1 lb (500 g) boneless, skinless turkey breast meat, cut into 1½-inch (4-cm) chunks

2 tablespoons peanut or vegetable oil

¼ lb (125 g) sugar snap peas or snow peas (mangetouts)

1 cup (4 oz/125 g) canned water chestnuts, rinsed, well drained and sliced

*T*o make the sauce, combine the orange juice and zest, soy sauce, ginger, garlic, shallot, honey and mustard in a small bowl and stir to mix well. Set aside.

To make the marinade, combine the egg white, mirin or sake, soy sauce and cornstarch in a bowl and stir to dissolve the cornstarch. Add the turkey pieces and toss to coat evenly. Set aside.

In a wok or frying pan over high heat, warm 1 tablespoon of the oil, swirling to coat the bottom and sides of the pan. When the oil is very hot but not quite smoking, add the peas and stir and toss every 15–20 seconds until just tender, 2–3 minutes. Add the water chestnuts and stir and toss for 1 minute longer. Transfer to a dish and set aside.

Reduce the heat to medium-high. Add the remaining 1 tablespoon oil to the pan, again swirling to coat the pan. When the oil is hot, add the turkey pieces and stir and toss every 15–20 seconds until firm and no trace of pink remains, 4–5 minutes. Be sure to distribute the turkey evenly in the pan so it comes into maximum contact with the heat and cooks evenly.

Quickly stir the reserved sauce and add to the pan over medium-high heat. Bring to a simmer and stir and toss until the sauce thickens slightly, 1–2 minutes. Return the peas and water chestnuts to the pan and toss to coat with the sauce. Cook for 1 minute longer.

Taste and adjust the seasonings. Serve immediately.

Serves 4

25

Chicken and Vegetables with Pesto

3 tablespoons peanut or vegetable oil

1 lb (500 g) boneless, skinless chicken breasts, cut into 1½-inch (4-cm) chunks

1 yellow onion, thinly sliced

1 red bell pepper (capsicum), seeded, deribbed and thinly sliced

2 small zucchini (courgettes), cut into strips 2 inches (5 cm) long, ¾ inch (2 cm) wide and ½ inch (12 mm) thick

½ lb (250 g) fresh mushrooms, sliced ¼ inch (6 mm) thick

¼ cup (2 fl oz/60 ml) chicken stock

½ cup (4 fl oz/125 ml) basil pesto

½ teaspoon salt

¼ teaspoon pepper

This Italian-inspired, brightly colored stir-fry tastes wonderful spooned over pasta or rice. Use your own favorite recipe for pesto, or purchase a high-quality product at a food store.

*I*n a wok or frying pan over high heat, warm 2 tablespoons of the oil, swirling to coat the bottom and sides of the pan. When the oil is very hot but not quite smoking, add the chicken pieces and stir and toss every 15–20 seconds until lightly browned and just cooked through, 4–6 minutes. Be sure to distribute the chicken evenly in the pan so it comes into maximum contact with the heat and cooks evenly. Transfer to a dish and set aside.

Add the remaining 1 tablespoon oil to the pan over medium-high heat, again swirling to coat the pan. When the oil is hot, add the onion and stir and toss every 15–20 seconds until it begins to soften, about 2 minutes. Add the bell pepper, zucchini and mushrooms and stir and toss every 15–20 seconds until the onion is tender, 3–4 minutes longer. Return the chicken to the pan, add the stock and stir and toss just until the chicken and stock are heated through, 2–3 minutes.

Remove from the heat, add the pesto, salt and pepper and toss until the chicken and vegetables are nicely coated with the sauce. Taste and adjust the seasonings. Serve immediately.

Serves 4

Beef, Asparagus and Red Bell Peppers

3 tablespoons peanut or vegetable oil
½ lb (250 g) asparagus, trimmed, cut
   on the diagonal into 1½-inch (4-cm)
   lengths (about 1½ cups), parboiled in
   boiling water for 2 minutes, drained,
   rinsed in cold water and drained
   again
1 lb (500 g) flank steak, sliced in half
   horizontally and then cut into thin
   strips 2 inches (5 cm) long and
   ¼ inch (6 mm) wide
1 red bell pepper (capsicum), seeded,
   deribbed and cut into strips 2 inches
   (5 cm) long and ¼ inch (6 mm) wide
2 teaspoons cornstarch dissolved in
   3 tablespoons water
all-purpose stir-fry sauce (*recipe on*
   page 12)

Tender flank steak is accented with green asparagus and red bell peppers, all bound together in a simple soy-and-ginger sauce. You can substitute turkey breast meat for the beef, if you prefer. Serve with steamed white rice (recipe on page 12).

*I*n a wok or frying pan over high heat, warm 1 tablespoon of the oil, swirling to coat the bottom and sides of the pan. When the oil is very hot but not quite smoking, add the asparagus and stir and toss every 10–15 seconds until lightly browned, about 2 minutes. Transfer to a dish.

Add another 1 tablespoon oil to the pan over high heat, again swirling to coat the pan. When the oil is hot but not quite smoking, add half of the beef strips and stir and toss every 15–20 seconds until lightly browned but still slightly pink inside, 2–3 minutes. Be sure to distribute the meat evenly in the pan so it comes into maximum contact with the heat and cooks evenly. Transfer to a bowl. Add the remaining 1 tablespoon oil to the pan and cook the remaining beef in the same manner.

Return the first batch of beef to the pan and add the bell pepper. Stir and toss over high heat until just beginning to wilt, 1–2 minutes. Quickly stir the cornstarch liquid and add it to the pan along with the stir-fry sauce. Cook, tossing the mixture occasionally, until the sauce thickens, 1–2 minutes. Return the asparagus to the pan, toss to coat evenly with the sauce and serve immediately.

Serves 4

Minced Chicken in Lettuce Cups

1 lb (500 g) ground (minced) chicken
1 tablespoon soy sauce
1 tablespoon natural rice vinegar
1 teaspoon Asian sesame oil
peanut or vegetable oil for deep-frying
1 oz (30 g) dried rice vermicelli noodles

FOR THE SAUCE:
2½ tablespoons soy sauce
1 tablespoon natural rice vinegar
1 teaspoon sugar
1 teaspoon Asian sesame oil
1 tablespoon hoisin sauce
1 teaspoon cornstarch

1 red bell pepper (capsicum), seeded,
   deribbed and very finely chopped
2 green (spring) onions, including
   tender green tops, finely chopped
2 teaspoons finely chopped, peeled
   fresh ginger
1 cup (4 oz/125 g) water chestnuts,
   rinsed, well drained and coarsely
   chopped
1 head iceberg or romaine lettuce,
   leaves separated into 6–8 individual
   "cups"

This dish can also be served family style, with the lettuce cups on a platter and the filling in a bowl, so that guests fill their own.

❧

*I*n a bowl, combine the chicken, soy sauce, vinegar and sesame oil and stir to mix well. Set aside.

In a wok or deep frying pan over high heat, pour in peanut or vegetable oil to a depth of 3 inches (7.5 cm) and heat until it registers 375°F (190°C) on a deep-fat thermometer, or until smoking. To test, drop in a piece of noodle; it should puff up within 1–2 seconds. Add the noodles and fry until puffed and just barely golden on the first side, 1–2 seconds. Using a slotted spoon, turn the noodles over and cook briefly on the second side. Using the spoon, transfer to paper towels to drain. Let the oil cool slightly, then strain through a fine-mesh sieve into a heatproof container.

To make the sauce, combine all the ingredients and stir to dissolve the cornstarch. Set aside.

Return the pan to high heat. Add 3 tablespoons of the reserved oil, swirling to coat the bottom and sides. (Reserve the remaining oil for deep-frying noodles or other foods.) When the oil is very hot but not quite smoking, add the chicken and stir and toss every 15–20 seconds until no longer pink, 1–2 minutes. Push it to the side of the pan. Add the bell pepper, green onions, ginger and water chestnuts and stir and toss for 1 minute. Quickly stir the reserved sauce and add to the pan. Stir and toss every 10–15 seconds until slightly thickened, about 1 minute. Remove from the heat and mix in the noodles, reserving a few for garnish.

Place the lettuce cups on individual plates; divide the chicken mixture among them. Top with the reserved noodles and serve.

Serves 3 or 4 as a main course, or 6–8 as a first course

Turkey Breast, Green Beans and Toasted Almonds

½ cup (2½ oz/75 g) slivered blanched almonds

3 tablespoons peanut or vegetable oil

1 lb (500 g) boneless, skinless turkey breast meat, cut into thin strips 2 inches (5 cm) long and ½ inch (12 mm) wide

3 celery stalks, cut into thin strips 2 inches (5 cm) long and ¼ inch (6 mm) wide

½ lb (250 g) green beans, trimmed and cut into 2-inch (5-cm) lengths, parboiled in boiling water for 3 minutes, drained, rinsed in cold water and drained again

2 teaspoons cornstarch dissolved in 3 tablespoons water

all-purpose stir-fry sauce (recipe on page 12)

This quick main course is full of crunch from the almonds and sweetness from the green beans. Select small, tender green beans for the best flavor and texture.

*I*n a dry wok or frying pan over medium-high heat, add the slivered almonds and toss constantly until evenly toasted, 1–2 minutes. Watch carefully so they do not burn. Transfer to a dish and set aside.

Raise the heat to high and add 2 tablespoons of the oil, swirling to coat the bottom and sides of the pan. When the oil is very hot but not quite smoking, add the turkey strips and stir and toss every 15–20 seconds until lightly browned and cooked through and no trace of pink remains, 4–5 minutes. Be sure to distribute the turkey evenly in the pan so it comes into maximum contact with the heat and cooks evenly. Transfer to another dish.

Add the remaining 1 tablespoon oil to the pan, again swirling to coat the pan. When the oil is hot, add the celery and stir and toss every 15–20 seconds until tender-crisp, 2–3 minutes. Add the green beans and stir and toss a few times for 1 minute longer. Quickly stir the cornstarch mixture and add it to the pan along with the stir-fry sauce and the turkey. Bring the liquid to a simmer and cook, tossing occasionally, until it begins to thicken, 2–3 minutes. Sprinkle on the toasted almonds, stir to mix and serve immediately.

Serves 4

Pork Tenderloin with Corn, Mushrooms and Carrots

FOR THE MARINADE:

2 cloves garlic, minced

1 tablespoon soy sauce

2 tablespoons sake

1 tablespoon cornstarch

1 lb (500 g) pork tenderloin, cut into
thin strips 2 inches (5 cm) long and
½ inch (12 mm) wide

3 tablespoons peanut or vegetable oil

2 small carrots, peeled and cut into thin
strips 2 inches (5 cm) long and
½ inch (12 mm) wide

½ lb (250 g) fresh oyster mushrooms,
tough stem bottoms removed and cut
into thin strips 2 inches (5 cm) long
and ¼ inch (6 mm) wide

2 ears of corn, kernels removed (about
1 cup/6 oz/185 g)

⅓ cup (3 fl oz/80 ml) beef stock

½ teaspoon salt

¼ teaspoon pepper

½ teaspoon chili oil, or to taste *(recipe
on page 13)*

1 tablespoon finely chopped fresh
cilantro (fresh coriander)

Serve as a main dish accompanied with your favorite noodles or rice.

To make the marinade, combine the garlic, soy sauce, sake and cornstarch in a bowl and stir to dissolve the cornstarch. Add the pork strips and toss to coat well. Cover and marinate in the refrigerator for 15 minutes to 1 hour.

In a wok or frying pan over high heat, warm 1 tablespoon of the peanut or vegetable oil, swirling to coat the bottom and sides of the pan. When the oil is very hot but not quite smoking, using a slotted spoon, remove half of the pork from the marinade and add it to the pan. Stir and toss every 15–20 seconds until golden brown, 3–4 minutes. Be sure to distribute the meat evenly in the pan so it comes into maximum contact with the heat and cooks evenly. Transfer to a dish. Add another 1 tablespoon oil to the pan and cook the remaining pork in the same manner. Transfer to the dish.

Add the remaining 1 tablespoon oil to the pan over high heat, again swirling to coat the pan. When the oil is very hot but not quite smoking, add the carrots and mushrooms and stir and toss every 15–20 seconds until just slightly softened, 2–3 minutes. Add the corn and stir and toss for 1 minute longer. Add the reserved pork with its accumulated juices, the beef stock, salt, pepper, chili oil and cilantro and stir and toss until heated through, about 1 minute. Taste and adjust the seasonings. Serve immediately.

Serves 4

Chicken Fajitas

3 tablespoons vegetable or olive oil

1 lb (500 g) boneless, skinless chicken breasts, cut into strips 2 inches (5 cm) long, ¾ inch (2 cm) wide and ¼ inch (6 mm) thick

1 red (Spanish) onion, thinly sliced

1 red bell pepper (capsicum), seeded, deribbed and thinly sliced

2 fresh jalapeño chili peppers, seeded and minced

2 cloves garlic, minced

1 tomato, peeled and diced

3 tablespoons fresh lime juice

½ teaspoon ground cumin

2 tablespoons chopped fresh cilantro (fresh coriander), plus fresh cilantro leaves for garnish

salt and pepper

FOR SERVING:

warmed flour or corn tortillas

1 cup (8 fl oz/250 ml) sour cream

1 cup (8 fl oz/250 ml) fresh tomato salsa

1 ripe avocado, halved, pitted, peeled and diced

Traditionally, fajitas are cooked on a grill. Here they're quickly stir-fried into a tasty tangle of colorful vegetables and chicken that forms a pretty filling for warm tortillas. If you can find them, use chicken "tenders," or tenderloins—strips of tender breast meat sold separately by weight in some meat markets.

*I*n a wok or frying pan over medium-high heat, warm 2 tablespoons of the oil, swirling to coat the bottom and sides of the pan. When the oil is hot, add the chicken strips and stir and toss every 15–20 seconds until lightly brown and just cooked through, 3–4 minutes. Be sure to distribute the chicken evenly in the pan so it comes into maximum contact with the heat and cooks evenly. Transfer to a dish and set aside.

Add the remaining 1 tablespoon oil to the pan, again swirling to coat the pan. Add the onion and stir and toss for 1 minute. Add the bell pepper and jalapeños and stir and toss every 15–20 seconds until the onion has softened, 4–6 minutes. Add the garlic and tomato and stir and toss for 1 minute longer. Add the lime juice, cumin, the 2 table-spoons chopped cilantro and the reserved chicken. Bring to a boil and cook for 1 minute. Add salt and pepper to taste.

Transfer to a serving bowl and garnish with cilantro leaves. Serve immediately with a basket of warmed tortillas and small bowls of the sour cream, salsa and avocado on the side.

Serves 4

Lemon-Orange Chicken

4 cups (32 fl oz/1 l) water

1½ lb (750 g) boneless, skinless chicken
  breasts, cut into strips 2½ inches
  (6 cm) long, ¾ inch (2 cm) wide
  and ¼ (6 mm) thick

2 tablespoons peanut or vegetable oil

2 teaspoons finely chopped, peeled
  fresh ginger

4 cloves garlic, minced

1 tablespoon cornstarch dissolved in
  1 tablespoon water

1 tablespoon finely shredded lemon zest

1 tablespoon finely shredded orange
  zest

½ cup (4 fl oz/125 ml) fresh lemon
  juice

½ cup (4 fl oz/125 ml) fresh orange
  juice

2 tablespoons sugar

2 tablespoons soy sauce

1 tablespoon Asian sesame oil

¼ cup (¾ oz/20 g) thinly sliced green
  (spring) onions, including tender
  green tops

*The secret to this lighter-than-usual citrus-flavored dish is
blanching the chicken briefly in water to create a velvety texture.*

*I*n a saucepan, bring the water to a boil. Immerse the
chicken strips in the boiling water for 2 minutes. Using a
slotted spoon or wire skimmer, transfer to a bowl. Discard
the water and set the chicken aside.

In a wok or frying pan over medium-high heat, warm the
peanut or vegetable oil, swirling to coat the bottom and
sides of the pan. When the oil is hot, add the ginger and
garlic and stir and toss for about 30 seconds. Quickly stir
the cornstarch mixture and add it to the pan along with
the lemon and orange zests and juices, sugar, soy sauce,
sesame oil and half of the green onions; bring to a boil.
Cook until slightly thickened, 1–2 minutes.

Add the chicken strips to the sauce and simmer until
cooked through, about 3 minutes longer.

Transfer to a serving bowl, garnish with the remaining
green onions and serve immediately.

Serves 4

Kung Pao Chicken

FOR THE SAUCE:
1 teaspoon cornstarch
¼ cup (2 fl oz/60 ml) chicken stock, preferably Chinese style *(recipe on page 13)*
1 teaspoon chili paste with garlic
2 tablespoons soy sauce
1 tablespoon dry sherry
1 teaspoon red wine vinegar
1 teaspoon sugar
1 teaspoon Asian sesame oil

FOR THE MARINADE:
1 tablespoon dry sherry
1 teaspoon soy sauce
1 egg white
1 tablespoon cornstarch

1½ lb (750 g) boneless, skinless chicken breasts, cut into ½-inch (12-mm) cubes
3 tablespoons peanut or vegetable oil
6–8 small dried red chili peppers, or to taste
½ cup (3 oz/90 g) unsalted roasted peanuts
1 teaspoon finely chopped, peeled fresh ginger
2 green (spring) onions, including tender green tops, cut on the diagonal into ½-inch (12-mm) slices

Cashews can be substituted for the peanuts in this Sichuan-inspired dish. Warn your guests not to eat the fiery chilies.

To make the sauce, stir together the cornstarch and chicken stock in a small bowl until the cornstarch dissolves. Add all the remaining sauce ingredients and stir well. Set aside.

To make the marinade, combine the sherry, soy sauce, egg white and cornstarch in a large bowl and stir to dissolve the cornstarch. Add the chicken pieces, toss well to coat and marinate for a few minutes at room temperature.

In a wok or frying pan over medium-high heat, warm 1 tablespoon of the peanut or vegetable oil, swirling to coat the bottom and sides. When the oil is hot, add the chilies and peanuts and stir and toss until the chilies are dark red and the peanuts are golden brown, about 2 minutes. Transfer to a bowl.

Add another 1 tablespoon oil to the pan over medium-high heat, again swirling to coat the pan. When the oil is hot, add half of the chicken and stir and toss every 15–20 seconds until golden brown and just cooked through, 4–5 minutes. Be sure to distribute the chicken evenly in the pan so it comes into maximum contact with the heat and cooks evenly. Transfer to a dish. Add the remaining 1 tablespoon oil to the pan and cook the remaining chicken in the same manner.

Return the peanuts, chilies and chicken to the pan, along with the ginger and green onions. Stir and toss for 1 minute. Quickly stir the reserved sauce and add it to the pan. Stir and toss over medium-high heat until the sauce begins to thicken, 1–2 minutes. Serve immediately.

Serves 4

Spicy Beef Salad

FOR THE DRESSING:

1 tablespoon Dijon mustard

2 teaspoons soy sauce

3 tablespoons natural rice vinegar

salt and pepper

⅓ cup (3 fl oz/80 ml) olive oil

1 tablespoon dry sherry

1 lb (500 g) flank steak, sliced in half
   horizontally and then cut into thin
   strips 2 inches (5 cm) long and
   ½ inch (12 mm) wide

1 head escarole or red-leaf lettuce,
   carefully washed, dried and torn into
   bite-sized pieces

1 bunch spinach, carefully washed,
   dried and torn into bite-sized pieces

3–4 tablespoons (1½–2 fl oz/45–60 ml)
   peanut or vegetable oil

½ red (Spanish) onion, finely chopped

1 tablespoon finely chopped, peeled
   fresh ginger

2 cloves garlic, minced

1 ear of corn, kernels removed (about
   ½ cup/3 oz/90 g)

1 tablespoon soy sauce

cherry tomato halves for garnish

½–1 teaspoon chili oil, or more to taste
   (recipe on page 13)

*Serve this as a refreshing main-course salad. Those who like their
food spicy should be generous with the chili oil.*

To make the dressing, whisk together the mustard, soy sauce,
vinegar and salt and pepper to taste in a small bowl. Gradually
whisk in the olive oil until well blended. Set aside.

In a large bowl, combine the sherry and beef strips, tossing to
coat evenly. Marinate for 15 minutes at room temperature.

In a large bowl, toss together the escarole or lettuce and
spinach with the dressing until evenly coated. Divide the salad
mixture evenly among 6 dinner plates and set aside.

In a wok or frying pan over high heat, warm 2 tablespoons of
the peanut or vegetable oil, swirling to coat. When very hot but
not quite smoking, add the onion and ginger and stir and toss
until the onion begins to soften, 2–3 minutes. Add the garlic
and cook for 30 seconds longer. Transfer to a bowl.

Add another 1 tablespoon oil to the pan over high heat, again
swirling to coat the pan. When the oil is hot but not quite
smoking, add half of the beef strips and stir and toss every
15–20 seconds until tender but still pink inside, 2–3 minutes.
Be sure to distribute the beef evenly in the pan so it comes into
maximum contact with the heat and cooks evenly. Transfer to
the bowl holding the onion mixture. Add the remaining 1
tablespoon oil, if needed, to the pan and cook the remaining
beef in the same manner. Transfer to the bowl.

Add the corn kernels and soy sauce to the pan over medium-
high heat and stir and toss until the corn is just tender, 1–2
minutes. Return the beef-onion mixture to the pan, stir and
heat through, about 30 seconds.

Spoon the mixture atop the greens. Garnish with cherry
tomato halves, drizzle with chili oil and serve.

Serves 6

Red Snapper with Tangerine-Chili Sauce

Here, a light citrus sauce is enlivened with chopped fresh chilies. Serve with celery, zucchini and carrots with red onion (recipe on page 97) and steamed white rice (page 12).

FOR THE SAUCE:

1 small fresh jalapeño pepper, seeded and minced

1 tablespoon finely shredded tangerine or orange zest

3 tablespoons fresh tangerine or orange juice

2 tablespoons soy sauce

1 tablespoon water

1 teaspoon natural rice vinegar

½ teaspoon fresh coarsely ground black pepper

1 teaspoon Asian sesame oil

¼ teaspoon sugar

1 lb (500 g) red snapper fillets, cut into strips 2 inches (5 cm) long and 1 inch (2.5 cm) wide

1 tablespoon soy sauce

3 tablespoons peanut or vegetable oil

3 cloves garlic, minced

2 teaspoons finely chopped, peeled fresh ginger

¼ lb (125 g) snow peas (mangetouts)

1 red bell pepper (capsicum), seeded, deribbed and cut into thin strips 2 inches (5 cm) long

*T*o make the sauce, combine the jalapeño pepper, tangerine or orange zest and juice, soy sauce, water, vinegar, black pepper, sesame oil and sugar in a bowl. Stir well and set aside.

In another bowl, toss together the fish strips and soy sauce.

In a wok or frying pan over high heat, warm 1 tablespoon of the peanut or vegetable oil, swirling to coat the bottom and sides of the pan. When the oil is very hot but not quite smoking, add half of the fish strips and stir and toss every 15–20 seconds until firm and slightly golden, 3–4 minutes. Be sure to distribute the fish evenly in the pan so it comes into maximum contact with the heat and cooks evenly. Transfer to a dish. Add another 1 tablespoon oil to the pan and cook the remaining fish strips in the same manner. Transfer to the dish.

Add the remaining 1 tablespoon oil to the pan over medium-high heat, again swirling to coat the pan. When the oil is hot, add the garlic and ginger and stir and toss briefly, then add the snow peas and bell pepper. Stir and toss every 15–20 seconds until the snow peas are tender-crisp, 1–2 minutes.

Quickly stir the reserved sauce and add it to the pan over medium-high heat along with the fish. Stir and toss until the fish is heated through and coated with the sauce, about 1 minute. Taste and adjust the seasonings. Serve immediately.

Serves 4

Crab in Tomato and Garlic Sauce

2 tablespoons olive oil

2 shallots, finely chopped

3 cloves garlic, minced

2 large tomatoes, peeled, seeded and finely chopped

½ cup (4 fl oz/125 ml) dry white wine

1 cooked crab, about 2 lb (1 kg), cracked (see note)

2 tablespoons finely chopped fresh parsley

salt and pepper

Ask the fishmonger to clean and crack the crab for you, dividing the body into quarters. Serve this dish with pasta or steamed white rice (recipe on page 12).

*I*n a wok or frying pan over medium-high heat, warm the olive oil, swirling to coat the bottom and sides of the pan. When the oil is hot, add the shallots and garlic and stir and toss every 10–15 seconds for 1 minute. Add the tomatoes and wine, bring to a boil and cook, stirring, for 2 minutes.

Add the crab pieces and stir and toss them in the sauce until the crab is coated with the sauce and completely heated through, 2–3 minutes.

Add the parsley and salt and pepper to taste and stir to mix. Serve immediately.

Serves 2

Quick Pot Stickers

FOR THE FILLING:

½ lb (250 g) medium-sized shrimp
(prawns), peeled, deveined and
finely chopped

½ lb (250 g) ground (minced) turkey
or pork

2 green (spring) onions, including
tender green tops, finely chopped

1 cup (3 oz/90 g) finely chopped
Chinese cabbage

2 cloves garlic, minced

1 teaspoon finely chopped, peeled
fresh ginger

2 tablespoons soy sauce

1 tablespoon dry sherry

pinch of pepper

1 package (10 oz/310 g) pot sticker
wrappers (48 wrappers; see note)

4 tablespoons (2 fl oz/60 ml) peanut or
vegetable oil

1 cup (8 fl oz/240 ml) Chinese-style
chicken stock (recipe on page 13)

FOR THE DIPPING SAUCE:

½ cup (4 fl oz/125 ml) soy sauce

5 tablespoons (2½ oz/75 ml) balsamic
vinegar

2 teaspoons finely chopped, peeled
fresh ginger

2 teaspoons Asian sesame oil or
1 teaspoon chili oil (recipe on page 13)

Look for packages labeled either "wrappers for pot stickers" or for gyoza, the Japanese equivalent of Chinese pot stickers. Pot stickers can be frozen for up to 1 month; do not thaw before cooking.

To make the filling, combine the shrimp and the turkey or pork, green onions, cabbage, garlic, ginger, soy sauce, sherry and pepper in a bowl and mix well.

For each pot sticker, transfer a wrapper to a work surface. Put 1 rounded teaspoon filling in the center. Fold the wrapper in half and press together firmly to form a fully sealed edge ½ inch (12 mm) wide. Using your thumb and forefinger, form 3 evenly spaced pleats along the sealed edge so there are 3 distinct indentations. Place the pot sticker seam-side up, flattening the bottom slightly so it stands upright, on a floured baking sheet and cover with a damp kitchen towel. Repeat until all the filling is used.

Preheat an oven to 300°F (150°C). In a wok or frying pan over medium-high heat, heat 1 tablespoon of the peanut or vegetable oil. When hot, arrange 12 pot stickers in the pan, seam-side up. Fry uncovered for about 5 minutes. As the pot stickers in the center brown, move them to the edges and move the less browned ones into the center so all cook evenly. Add ¼ cup (2 fl oz/60 ml) of the stock, cover, reduce the heat to low and cook for 10 minutes longer. Uncover and cook until all the liquid evaporates, 2–3 minutes longer. Transfer to a platter and keep warm in the oven. Cook the remaining pot stickers in the same manner with the remaining oil and stock.

Meanwhile, in a bowl, combine all the sauce ingredients and stir well. Divide among individual bowls. Serve the pot stickers immediately with the dipping sauce.

Makes about 48 pot stickers; serves 6–8

Crab with Black Bean Sauce

2 tablespoons peanut or vegetable oil

2 cloves garlic, minced

1 teaspoon finely chopped, peeled
fresh ginger

2 tablespoons salted and fermented
black beans, rinsed and drained

1 tablespoon soy sauce

1 tablespoon dry sherry

½ cup (4 fl oz/125 ml) chicken stock,
preferably Chinese style *(recipe on
page 13)*

2 green (spring) onions, including
tender green tops, finely chopped

1 cooked crab, about 2 lb (1 kg),
cracked *(see note)*

Ask the fishmonger to clean and crack the crab for you. The legs should be left whole and the body divided into quarters. Chinese salted and fermented black beans are usually sold in small plastic bags; look for them in Asian shops and well-stocked food stores. Be sure to rinse the beans before using because they are quite salty. Vegetable fried rice (recipe on page 63) makes a nice accompaniment.

*I*n a wok or frying pan over medium-high heat, warm the oil, swirling to coat the bottom and sides of the pan. When the oil is hot, add the garlic and ginger and stir and toss every 10–15 seconds for 1 minute. Add the black beans, soy sauce, sherry, stock and green onions, bring to a boil and cook for 2 minutes.

Add the crab pieces and stir and toss them in the sauce until the crab is coated with the sauce and completely heated through, 2–3 minutes.

Taste and adjust the seasonings. Serve immediately.

Serves 2

Crispy Fish in Sweet-and-Sour Sauce

FOR THE SAUCE:

2 teaspoons cornstarch

¼ cup (2 fl oz/60 ml) water

3 tablespoons chicken stock

1½ tablespoons soy sauce

2 tablespoons dry sherry

1 tablespoon tomato paste

3 tablespoons fresh orange juice

2 tablespoons natural rice vinegar

1½ tablespoons sugar

1 egg white

2 tablespoons cornstarch

1 teaspoon all-purpose (plain) flour,
plus flour for dusting plate

½ teaspoon baking powder

1 lb (500 g) firm white fish fillets, such
as turbot or halibut, cut into pieces
2 inches (5 cm) long and 1 inch
(2.5 cm) wide

6 tablespoons (3 fl oz/90 ml) peanut or
vegetable oil

fresh parsley sprigs, optional

This dish goes well with three-color fried rice (recipe on page 72) or spinach with garlic (page 82).

*T*o make the sauce, stir together the cornstarch and water in a small bowl until the cornstarch dissolves. Add the chicken stock, soy sauce, sherry, tomato paste, orange juice, vinegar and sugar and stir together until smooth. Set aside.

In another small bowl, whisk the egg white until frothy, about 10 seconds. In yet another bowl, stir together the cornstarch, the 1 teaspoon flour and the baking powder. Lightly flour a large plate. Dip each fish piece in the egg white and then dredge it in the cornstarch-flour mixture. Place on the plate.

In a wok or frying pan over high heat, warm 4 tablespoons (2 fl oz/60 ml) of the oil, swirling to coat the bottom and sides of the pan. When the oil is very hot but not quite smoking, add half of the fish pieces and cook for 1½–2 minutes on the first side. Using tongs, turn the fish over and cook until firm and cooked through, 1½–2 minutes longer. As the fish cooks, holding the pan handle firmly with a pot holder, quickly rotate the pan so the oil swirls around the fish. Again using tongs, transfer the cooked fish to a warmed platter. Cover loosely. Add the remaining 2 tablespoons oil to the pan and cook the remaining fish in the same manner. Transfer to the platter.

Discard the oil in the pan. Quickly stir the reserved sauce and add it to the pan over medium heat. Cook until it just begins to thicken, about 30 seconds. Taste and adjust the seasonings.

Drizzle the sauce over the fish, garnish with the parsley sprigs (if desired) and serve immediately.

Serves 4

Scallops with Zucchini and Mushrooms

4 tablespoons (2 fl oz/60 ml) peanut or vegetable oil

4 small zucchini (courgettes), cut into thin strips 2 inches (5 cm) long and ½ inch (12 mm) wide

6 fresh mushrooms, thinly sliced

3 cloves garlic, minced

1¼ lb (625 g) scallops (*see note*)

½ teaspoon salt

¼ teaspoon pepper

2 tablespoons fresh lemon juice

1 tablespoon chopped fresh parsley

lemon slices for garnish, optional

Small bay scallops or larger sea scallops can be used. If using sea scallops, slice them vertically. If using bay scallops, leave whole. A mixed green salad and your favorite rice dish will round out this simple main course.

*I*n a wok or frying pan over medium-high heat, warm 2 tablespoons of the oil, swirling to coat the bottom and sides of the pan. When the oil is hot, add the zucchini and mushrooms and stir and toss until both are tender-crisp, 2–3 minutes. Add the garlic and stir and toss for 1 minute longer. Transfer to a bowl and set aside.

Add another 1 tablespoon oil to the pan over medium-high heat, again swirling to coat the pan. When the oil is hot, add half of the scallops and stir and toss every 15–20 seconds until just tender, 2–3 minutes. Be sure to distribute the scallops evenly in the pan so they come into maximum contact with the heat and cook evenly. Transfer to the bowl holding the vegetables. Add the remaining 1 tablespoon oil to the pan and cook the remaining scallops in the same manner.

Return the first batch of scallops to the pan, along with the zucchini and mushrooms. Stir and toss gently until just heated through, about 30 seconds. Add the salt, pepper and lemon juice and stir and toss to incorporate. Taste and adjust the seasonings. Transfer to a serving dish, sprinkle with the parsley, garnish with lemon slices (if desired) and serve immediately.

Serves 4

Shrimp and Leeks with Toasted Pine Nuts

3 tablespoons pine nuts

3 tablespoons peanut or vegetable oil

4 leeks, white part only, carefully washed and cut into pieces 2 inches (5 cm) long and then lengthwise into thin slivers

2 teaspoons finely chopped, peeled fresh ginger

3 garlic cloves, minced

2 lb (1 kg) medium-sized shrimp (prawns), peeled and deveined

¼ cup (2 fl oz/60 ml) dry sherry

¼ cup (2 fl oz/60 ml) soy sauce

1 tablespoon Asian sesame oil

1 teaspoon chili oil, or to taste (recipe on page 13)

salt and pepper

The sweetness of sautéed leeks blends beautifully with the mildness of the shrimp. Serve this with vegetable fried rice (recipe on page 63) or steamed white rice (page 12).

In a dry wok or frying pan over medium heat, toast the pine nuts, stirring constantly until lightly browned, 1–2 minutes. Watch carefully so they do not burn. Transfer to a bowl and set aside.

Raise the heat to high and add 2 tablespoons of the peanut or vegetable oil, swirling to coat the bottom and sides of the pan. When the oil is very hot but not quite smoking, add the leeks and stir and toss until wilted, 6–7 minutes. Be sure to distribute the leeks evenly in the pan so they come into maximum contact with the heat and cook evenly. Add the ginger and garlic and stir and toss until they are softened, about 1 minute longer. Transfer to a dish.

Add the remaining 1 tablespoon oil to the pan over high heat, again swirling to coat the pan. When the oil is hot but not quite smoking, add the shrimp and stir and toss every 15–20 seconds until they turn pink and are firm, 3–4 minutes. Be sure to distribute the shrimp evenly in the pan so they come into maximum contact with the heat and cook evenly. Add the sherry, soy sauce and the reserved leeks and bring to a boil, stirring and tossing to mix well. Add the toasted pine nuts, sesame oil, chili oil, and salt and pepper to taste and stir and toss for 1 minute longer.

Taste and adjust the seasonings. Serve immediately.

Serves 4–6

Swordfish, Sugar Snap Peas and Carrots in Lime Sauce

FOR THE SAUCE:
⅓ cup (3 fl oz/80 ml) fresh lime juice
1 clove garlic, minced
1 tablespoon finely chopped fresh
    cilantro (fresh coriander)
dash of chili oil *(recipe on page 13)*
2 teaspoons lemon or lime marmalade
¼ teaspoon salt

FOR THE MARINADE:
1 egg white
1 tablespoon sake
2 teaspoons soy sauce
1 tablespoon cornstarch

1 lb (500 g) swordfish fillets, about
    ¾ inch (2 cm) thick, cut into ¾-inch
    (2-cm) chunks
4 tablespoons (2 fl oz/60 ml) peanut or
    vegetable oil
2 green (spring) onions, including
    tender green tops, finely chopped
1 teaspoon minced, peeled fresh ginger
¼ lb (125 g) sugar snap peas
2 small carrots, cut into thin strips
    2 inches (5 cm) long and ¼ inch
    (6 mm) wide

Swordfish is a firm, meaty fish that lends itself well to stir-frying. Snow peas (mangetouts) can be substituted for the sugar snap peas. Serve with simple stir-fried noodles or steamed white rice (recipe on page 12).

To make the sauce, combine the lime juice, garlic, cilantro, chili oil, lemon or lime marmalade and salt in a small bowl and stir to mix well. Set aside.

To make the marinade, combine the egg white, sake, soy sauce and cornstarch in a large bowl and stir to dissolve the cornstarch. Add the swordfish pieces; toss gently to coat. Set aside.

In a wok or frying pan over high heat, warm 2 tablespoons of the peanut or vegetable oil, swirling to coat the bottom and sides of the pan. When the oil is very hot but not quite smoking, add the green onions, ginger, sugar snap peas and carrots and stir and toss every 15–20 seconds until the vegetables are tender-crisp, 2–3 minutes. Transfer to a dish.

Add the remaining 2 tablespoons oil to the pan over high heat, again swirling to coat the pan. When the oil is hot but not quite smoking, add the swordfish and stir and toss gently every 15–20 seconds until firm and opaque, 2–3 minutes. Be sure to distribute the fish evenly in the pan so it comes into maximum contact with the heat and cooks evenly. Return the vegetables to the pan and stir and toss gently once or twice, cooking for about 30 seconds.

Quickly stir the reserved sauce and add it to the pan. Stir and toss to combine and heat through, about 1 minute longer. Taste and adjust the seasonings. Serve immediately.

Serves 2–3

Shrimp with Tomato-Basil Sauce

3 tablespoons olive oil
1 lb (500 g) medium-sized shrimp
  (prawns), peeled and deveined
2 shallots, finely chopped
3 cloves garlic, minced
2 large tomatoes, peeled, seeded and
  finely chopped
½ cup (4 fl oz/125 ml) dry white wine
2 tablespoons finely chopped fresh basil
salt and pepper

This Mediterranean-inspired dish is excellent accompanied with pasta. If you like, toss the pasta with garlic, olive oil and Parmesan cheese.

In a wok or frying pan over medium-high heat, warm 1 tablespoon of the olive oil, swirling to coat the bottom and sides of the pan. When the oil is hot, add half of the shrimp and stir and toss every 15–20 seconds until they turn pink and are firm, 3–4 minutes. Be sure to distribute the shrimp evenly in the pan so they come into maximum contact with the heat and cook evenly. Transfer to a bowl. Add another 1 tablespoon of the olive oil to the pan and cook the remaining shrimp in the same manner. Transfer to the bowl.

Add the remaining 1 tablespoon olive oil to the pan over medium-high heat, again swirling to coat the pan. When the oil is hot, add the shallots and garlic and stir and toss every 10–15 seconds for 1 minute. Add the tomatoes and wine, bring to a boil and cook, stirring occasionally, until the tomatoes are soft, 2–3 minutes. Add the basil and season to taste with salt and pepper.

Return the shrimp to the pan and stir and toss until the shrimp are coated with the sauce and heated through, about 1 minute. Taste and adjust the seasonings. Serve immediately.

Serves 4

Vegetable Fried Rice

3 cups (15 oz/470 g) cold steamed
white rice (recipe on page 12)

2 eggs

4 tablespoons (2 fl oz/60 ml) peanut or
vegetable oil

1 cup (2 oz/60 g) small broccoli florets

1 carrot, peeled and cut into 1-inch
(2.5-cm) pieces

6 fresh mushrooms, cut into slices
½ inch (12 mm) thick

1 teaspoon dry sherry

2 ears of corn, kernels removed (about
1 cup/6 oz/185 g)

¼ cup (2 fl oz/60 ml) chicken stock,
preferably Chinese style (recipe on
page 13)

2 tablespoons soy sauce

2 tablespoons thinly sliced green
(spring) onion, including tender
green tops

½ cup (3 oz/90 g) unsalted roasted
peanuts, optional

You can vary this recipe by using dried mushrooms in place of the fresh: Soak 6 dried shiitake (black) mushrooms in boiling water to cover for 20 minutes; drain, remove and discard the stems and cut the caps into slices ½ inch (12 mm) thick. Add to the pan with the broccoli.

*T*o separate the rice grains, place in a bowl. Rub the grains between wet fingers until they are separated. Set aside.

In a small bowl, beat the eggs lightly. In a wok or frying pan over medium heat, warm 1 tablespoon of the oil, swirling to coat the bottom and sides of the pan. When the oil is hot, add the eggs and stir continuously until soft curds form, about 1 minute. Transfer to a bowl and set aside.

Add another 1 tablespoon oil to the pan over medium-high heat, again swirling to coat. When hot, add the broccoli, carrot and mushrooms and stir and toss every 15–20 seconds until the vegetables just begin to soften, 2–3 minutes. Add the sherry and stir and toss for 1 minute. Add the corn and stir and toss for 1 minute longer. Add to the bowl holding the eggs.

Add the remaining 2 tablespoons oil to the pan over medium-high heat, again swirling to coat the pan. When the oil is hot, add the rice and stir and toss every 20–30 seconds until it is lightly browned, about 5 minutes. Add the stock, soy sauce and green onion and stir to combine. Add the reserved vegetables, eggs and the peanuts (if desired) and stir and toss until the egg is in small pieces and the mixture is heated through, about 1 minute longer.

Taste and adjust the seasonings. Serve immediately.

Serves 4–6

Pasta Primavera

1 cup (5 oz/155 g) shelled fresh green
  peas (about 1 lb/500 g unshelled) or
  thawed, frozen petite peas
5 tablespoons (3 fl oz/80 ml) fruity
  olive oil
4 shallots, finely chopped
2 zucchini (courgettes), cut into thin
  strips 2 inches (5 cm) long and
  ½ inch (12 mm) wide
2 carrots, peeled and cut into thin strips
  2 inches (5 cm) long and ½ inch
  (12 mm) wide
½ lb (250 g) fresh mushrooms, thinly
  sliced
¼ red bell pepper (capsicum), seeded,
  deribbed and cut into small dice
½ cup (3 oz/90 g) well-drained peeled,
  seeded and diced tomato (fresh or
  canned)
4 cloves garlic, minced
1 cup (8 fl oz/250 ml) chicken stock
4 tablespoons finely chopped fresh basil
1½ teaspoons salt
¼ teaspoon white pepper
1 tablespoon vegetable oil
¾ lb (375 g) dried angel hair pasta
3 oz (90 g) prosciutto, sliced ⅛ inch
  (3 mm) thick and coarsely chopped
½ cup (2 oz/60 g) freshly grated
  Parmesan cheese

*Here is a light, colorful version of a classic springtime pasta dish. A
simple green salad and some crusty French bread round out the meal.*

Bring a large pot three-fourths full of water to a boil. If using
fresh peas, add them to the water and boil until just tender,
about 5 minutes. Using a slotted spoon or wire skimmer,
transfer the peas to a bowl of cold water to stop the cooking.
Drain again and set aside. Keep the water at a boil.

In a wok or frying pan over medium heat, warm the olive oil,
swirling to coat the bottom and sides of the pan. When the oil
is hot, add the shallots and stir and toss every 20 seconds until
softened, about 3 minutes. Add the zucchini, carrots,
mushrooms and bell pepper and stir and toss every 20 seconds
until cooked but still tender-crisp, about 3 minutes.

Add the tomato, garlic, stock, basil, ½ teaspoon of the salt
and the white pepper to the pan and simmer uncovered until
slightly reduced, about 3 minutes.

While the sauce simmers, add the vegetable oil, the remaining
1 teaspoon salt and the pasta to the boiling water. Cook over
high heat, stirring often, until al dente, about 4 minutes.

Just before the pasta is ready, add the cooked fresh peas or
the thawed, frozen peas and the prosciutto to the sauce and stir
and toss until heated through, about 1 minute. Taste and adjust
the seasonings.

Drain the pasta well and mound on a warmed serving platter.
Pour the hot vegetable mixture over the pasta and toss to mix
well. Sprinkle with a little of the Parmesan cheese and serve
immediately. Pass the remaining cheese at the table.

Serves 6

Ants on a Tree

3 oz (90 g) cellophane noodles
2 tablespoons soy sauce
1 tablespoon dry sherry
1 teaspoon chili paste with garlic
1 teaspoon sugar
½ cup (4 fl oz/125 ml) beef stock
2 tablespoons peanut or vegetable oil
½ lb (250 g) ground (minced) pork
   or beef
2 green (spring) onions, including
   tender green tops, sliced
1 teaspoon minced, peeled fresh ginger
½ cup (2 oz/60 g) canned water
   chestnuts, rinsed, well drained and
   sliced

The funny name for this delicious Sichuanese main dish comes from the resemblance of the tiny bits of ground meat dotting glassy cellophane noodles to ants climbing on a tree trunk. The noodles, which are made from mung bean starch and which turn translucent when soaked, can be found in Asian shops and many well-stocked food markets. Accompany with a stir-fried green vegetable.

*P*lace the noodles in a large bowl and add boiling water to cover. Let stand for 20 minutes. Drain well and cut the noodles into 2-inch (5-cm) lengths. Spread out the noodles on a kitchen towel to absorb excess moisture.

In a small bowl, stir together the soy sauce, sherry, chili paste, sugar and stock. Set aside.

In a wok or frying pan over high heat, warm the oil, swirling to coat the bottom and sides of the pan. When the oil is very hot but not quite smoking, add the pork or beef and stir and toss every 15–20 seconds until no pinkness remains, 3–4 minutes.

Push the meat to one side of the pan, add the green onions and ginger and stir and toss for 30 seconds. Add the water chestnuts and stir and toss together all of the ingredients, including the meat, for 30 seconds longer.

Quickly stir the reserved soy mixture and add to the pan. Bring to a boil. Reduce the heat to medium-high and add the reserved noodles. Cook until the liquid is absorbed but the mixture is still moist, about 3 minutes longer. Taste and adjust the seasonings. Serve immediately.

Serves 4

Thai Noodles

6 oz (185 g) dried rice vermicelli
  noodles
4 tablespoons (2 fl oz/60 ml) peanut or
  vegetable oil
⅓ lb (170 g) medium-sized shrimp
  (prawns), peeled, deveined and cut
  into 1-inch (2.5-cm) pieces
3 cloves garlic, coarsely chopped
2 eggs, lightly beaten
1 tablespoon sugar
2 tablespoons fish sauce
1 cup (2 oz/60 g) bean sprouts
2 tablespoons coarsely chopped
  unsalted roasted peanuts
½ teaspoon red pepper flakes, or to
  taste
1 green (spring) onion, including tender
  green tops, coarsely chopped
2 limes, thinly sliced

Called pad Thai, *this dish is traditionally made with a dried flat noodle similar to linguine, but any dried rice noodle will do. Here, the more readily available rice vermicelli is used.*

Place the noodles in a bowl with warm water to cover. Let stand 15 minutes. Drain and spread on a baking sheet to dry.

Meanwhile, in a wok or frying pan over high heat, warm 1 tablespoon of the oil, swirling to coat the bottom and sides. When very hot but not quite smoking, add the shrimp and stir and toss every 10–15 seconds until pink and firm, about 1 minute. Add the garlic and stir and toss until fragrant, about 30 seconds longer. Transfer to a bowl and set aside.

Add another 1 tablespoon oil to the pan over medium-high heat, again swirling to coat. When hot, add the eggs and stir until soft curds form, about 1 minute. Add to the shrimp.

Add the remaining 2 tablespoons oil to the pan over medium-high heat, again swirling to coat. When hot, add the drained noodles. Be sure to distribute the noodles evenly in the pan so they come into maximum contact with the heat and cook evenly. Cook for 2–3 minutes. Using a spatula, flip them, again spreading evenly. Cook, stirring every 30 seconds, until browned on the second side, 2–3 minutes longer.

Push the noodles to the side of the pan and add the sugar and fish sauce over medium-high heat. When the sugar dissolves, using tongs or 2 large forks, toss the noodles with the sauce. Add half each of the bean sprouts and peanuts and the reserved shrimp mixture; stir and toss. Turn out onto a warmed serving platter. Garnish with the remaining bean sprouts and peanuts, the pepper flakes, green onion and lime slices, then serve.

Serves 4

Noodles with Spicy Peanut Sauce

FOR THE SAUCE:

⅔ cup (6 oz/185 g) smooth peanut
  butter
¼ cup (2 fl oz/60 ml) water
½ cup (4 fl oz/125 ml) soy sauce
2 tablespoons Asian sesame oil
2 tablespoons dry sherry
4 teaspoons natural rice vinegar
¼ cup (3 oz/90 g) honey
4 cloves garlic, minced
2 teaspoons minced, peeled fresh ginger
1 tablespoon chili oil, or to taste (recipe
  on page 13)

1 lb (500 g) fresh Chinese mein noodles
3 tablespoons peanut or vegetable oil
2 carrots, cut into thin strips 2 inches
  (5 cm) long and ¼ inch (6 mm) wide
4 green (spring) onions, including
  tender green tops, cut into 2-inch
  (5-cm) lengths and then halved
  lengthwise

You will need a regular or hand blender or a small food processor to mix the peanut sauce. Use Chinese mein noodles made without eggs; look for them in Asian markets and well-stocked food stores.

To make the sauce, combine the peanut butter, water, soy sauce, sesame oil, sherry, vinegar, honey, garlic, ginger and chili oil in a blender or in a small food processor fitted with the metal blade. Blend or process until well mixed and smooth. Set aside.

Bring a large pot three-fourths full of water to a boil. Add the noodles and boil for 2 minutes. Drain well and set aside.

In a wok or frying pan over high heat, warm 2 tablespoons of the peanut or vegetable oil, swirling to coat the bottom and sides of the pan. When the oil is very hot but not quite smoking, add the carrots and stir and toss every 15–20 seconds until just tender, 3–4 minutes. Add the green onions and stir and toss for 1 minute.

Push the carrot-onion mixture to the side of the pan and add the remaining 1 tablespoon oil over medium-high heat, again swirling to coat the pan. When the oil is hot, add the drained noodles and, using 2 tongs or 2 large forks, stir and toss every 15–20 seconds for 2 minutes, being careful to keep the noodles from sticking together and heating them evenly until very hot. Turn off the heat and immediately add the peanut sauce. Toss until the noodles and vegetables are evenly coated with the sauce.

Taste and adjust the seasonings. Serve immediately.

Serves 4–6

71

Three-Color Fried Rice

3 cups (15 oz/470 g) cold steamed
  white rice (recipe on page 12)
2 eggs
4 tablespoons (2 fl oz/60 ml) peanut or
  vegetable oil
¼ lb (125 g) medium-sized shrimp
  (prawns), peeled, deveined and
  coarsely chopped
1 teaspoon dry sherry
½ cup (½ oz/15 g) dried shiitake
  (black) mushrooms, soaked in boiling
  water to cover for 20 minutes,
  drained, stems discarded, and caps
  cut into ½-inch (12-mm) pieces
3 oz (90 g) Chinese-style barbecued
  pork, diced (about ½ cup)
½ cup (2½ oz/75 g) thawed, frozen
  petite peas
¼ cup (2 fl oz/60 ml) chicken stock,
  preferably Chinese style (recipe on
  page 13)
2 tablespoons soy sauce
2 tablespoons thinly sliced green
  (spring) onion, including tender
  green tops
½ cup (3 oz/90 g) unsalted roasted
  peanuts

This full-flavored dish is an ideal accompaniment to chicken with plum sauce (recipe on page 15). The barbecued pork (char siu) can be found in Chinese markets carrying cooked meats and other foods; or substitute cooked ham.

To separate the rice grains, place in a bowl. Wet your fingers and rub the rice between them until the grains are separated. Set aside.

In a small bowl, beat the eggs lightly. In a wok or frying pan over medium heat, warm 1 tablespoon of the oil, swirling to coat the bottom and sides of the pan. When the oil is hot, add the eggs and stir continuously until soft curds form, about 1 minute. Transfer to a bowl and set aside.

Add another 1 tablespoon oil to the pan over high heat, again swirling to coat the pan. When the oil is very hot but not quite smoking, add the shrimp and stir and toss every 15–20 seconds until pink, 1–2 minutes. Add the sherry and stir and toss for 1 minute longer. Transfer to the bowl holding the eggs.

Add the remaining 2 tablespoons oil to the pan over medium-high heat, again swirling to coat the pan. When the oil is hot, add the rice and stir and toss every 20–30 seconds until it is lightly browned, about 5 minutes. Add the mushrooms, pork, peas, stock, soy sauce and green onion and stir to combine. Add the shrimp, eggs and peanuts and stir and toss until the egg is in small pieces and all the ingredients are heated through, about 1 minute longer.

Taste and adjust the seasonings. Serve immediately.

Serves 6

Shrimp and Pork Chow Mein

½ lb (250 g) fresh Chinese mein
  noodles

FOR THE SAUCE:
3 tablespoons dry sherry
3 tablespoons soy sauce
1 teaspoon sugar
pepper

3½ tablespoons peanut or vegetable oil
¼ lb (125 g) pork tenderloin or fillet,
  cut into thin strips 2 inches (5 cm)
  long and ½ inch (12 mm) wide
¼ lb (125 g) small shrimp (prawns),
  peeled and deveined
6–8 fresh shiitake mushrooms, stems
  removed and caps cut into thin strips
1 small bok choy, pale green part and
  two-thirds of the white stalk, finely
  sliced on the diagonal
4 green (spring) onions, including
  tender green tops, finely chopped

Dried shiitake (black) mushrooms can be substituted for the fresh: Soak in boiling water for 20 minutes, drain, discard the stems and cut into thin strips.

*F*ill a large pot three-fourths full of water and bring to a boil. Add the noodles and boil until barely tender, 3–4 minutes; do not overcook. Drain well and set aside.

To make the sauce, combine the sherry, soy sauce, sugar and pepper to taste in a small bowl, stirring well. Set aside.

In a wok or frying pan over high heat, warm 2 tablespoons of the oil, swirling to coat the bottom and sides. When very hot but not quite smoking, add the pork and stir and toss for 1 minute. Add the shrimp and stir and toss every 15–20 seconds until the pork is firm and the shrimp are nearly cooked, 1–2 minutes longer. Add the mushrooms, bok choy and green onions and stir and toss every 15–20 seconds for 2–3 minutes. Cover and cook until the vegetables just begin to wilt, about 1 minute longer. Quickly stir the reserved sauce and add half of it to the pan; toss for 1 minute longer. Transfer to a dish and set aside; cover to keep warm.

Reduce the heat to medium and add the remaining 1½ tablespoons oil, again swirling to coat. When hot, add the remaining sauce mixture. Then add the drained noodles and toss gently every 15–20 seconds just until heated through, about 2 minutes. Raise the heat to high and return three-fourths of the shrimp-pork mixture to the pan. Using tongs or 2 large forks, stir and toss until well mixed and heated through, about 1 minute longer. Taste and adjust the seasonings.

Transfer to a warmed platter. Garnish with the reserved shrimp-pork mixture and serve.

Serves 2 as a main dish, or 4 as a side dish

Tofu-Vegetable Fried Rice

4 cups (1¼ lb/625 g) cold steamed
    white rice (*recipe on page 12*)
6 tablespoons (3 fl oz/90 ml) peanut or
    vegetable oil
2 eggs, lightly beaten
½ lb (250 g) tofu, cut into ½-inch
    (12-mm) cubes
1 tablespoon balsamic vinegar
1 leek, including tender green tops,
    carefully washed and finely chopped
1 cup (2 oz/60 g) small broccoli florets
1 carrot, peeled and cut into 1-inch
    (2.5-cm) pieces
1 zucchini (courgette), finely chopped
2 cups (6 oz/185 g) finely chopped
    Chinese cabbage
1 teaspoon dry sherry
¼ cup (2 fl oz/60 ml) chicken stock,
    preferably Chinese style (*recipe on
    page 13*)
2 tablespoons soy sauce
½ cup (2 oz/60 g) canned water
    chestnuts, rinsed, well drained and
    sliced
2 tablespoons thinly sliced green
    (spring) onions, including tender
    green tops

*Tofu, also known as bean curd, comes in soft and firm forms; select
the latter for this recipe.*

*T*o separate the rice grains, place in a bowl. Rub the grains
between wet fingers until they are separated. Set aside.

In a wok or frying pan over medium heat, warm 1 tablespoon
of the oil, swirling to coat the bottom and sides. When the oil
is hot, add the eggs and stir continuously until soft curds form,
about 1 minute. Transfer to a bowl and set aside.

Add another 1 tablespoon oil to the pan over medium-high heat,
again swirling to coat. When hot, add the tofu and stir and toss
every 20–30 seconds until it begins to brown, 4–5 minutes. Add
the vinegar; cook, stirring once, for 30 seconds. Add to the eggs.

Add another 1 tablespoon oil over medium-high heat, again
swirling to coat. When hot, add the leek and stir and toss until
slightly softened, 2–3 minutes. Add another 1 tablespoon oil to
the pan over medium-high heat, again swirling to coat. When
hot, add the broccoli, carrot, zucchini and cabbage to the leeks
and stir and toss every 15–20 seconds until they just begin to
soften, 2–3 minutes. Add the sherry and stir and toss for
1 minute longer. Add to the eggs and tofu.

Add the remaining 2 tablespoons oil to the pan over medium-
high heat, again swirling to coat. When hot, add the rice and
stir and toss every 20–30 seconds until lightly browned, about
5 minutes. Add the stock, soy sauce, water chestnuts and green
onions and stir to combine. Add the tofu, vegetables and egg
and stir and toss until the egg is in small pieces and the mixture
is heated through, about 1 minute longer. Taste and adjust the
seasonings. Serve immediately.

Serves 6–8

77

Crispy Noodles with Tricolored Vegetables

FOR THE SAUCE:

2 tablespoons cornstarch

3 tablespoons soy sauce

2 tablespoons dry sherry

2 tablespoons dark brown sugar

½ cup (4 fl oz/125 ml) chicken stock, preferably Chinese style (recipe on page 13)

2 teaspoons Asian sesame oil

pinch of red pepper flakes

½ cup (½ oz/15 g) dried shiitake (black) mushrooms, cut in half if large

1 package (8 oz/250 g) dried Chinese or Japanese wheat noodles

4 tablespoons (2 fl oz/60 ml) peanut or vegetable oil

6 green (spring) onions, including tender green tops, thinly sliced

1 tablespoon finely chopped, peeled fresh ginger

2 cloves garlic, minced

2 carrots, peeled and thinly sliced

½ lb (250 g) sugar snap peas

6 fresh mushrooms, thinly sliced

2 cups (12 oz/375 g) cubed, cooked chicken, beef or lamb

To make the sauce, combine the cornstarch, soy sauce, sherry, brown sugar, stock, sesame oil and red pepper flakes in a small bowl and stir to dissolve the cornstarch and sugar. Set aside.

Place the dried mushrooms in a bowl with boiling water to cover and let soften for 20 minutes.

Meanwhile, fill a large pot three-fourths full of water and bring to a boil. Add the noodles and boil until barely tender, 3–4 minutes; do not overcook. Drain well and spread out on a kitchen towel to absorb excess moisture.

Drain the mushrooms, reserving ½ cup (4 fl oz/125 ml) of the liquid. Stir the liquid into the sauce mixture. Remove the mushroom stems and discard; set the mushrooms aside.

In a wok or frying pan over high heat, warm 2 tablespoons of the peanut or vegetable oil, swirling to coat. When very hot but not quite smoking, add the noodles and toss with tongs or 2 large forks until crisp and golden, 3–5 minutes. Transfer to a bowl.

Heat the remaining 2 tablespoons oil in the pan over medium-high heat, again swirling to coat. When hot, add the green onions, ginger and garlic and stir and toss every 15–20 seconds until the onions begin to soften, 1–2 minutes. Add the carrots, peas and fresh mushrooms and continue to stir and toss until the vegetables are tender-crisp, about 3 minutes.

Quickly stir the reserved sauce and add it to the pan along with the shiitake mushrooms. Raise the heat to high, add the chicken or meat and stir and toss until heated through and the sauce is slightly thickened, 1–2 minutes. Taste and adjust the seasonings. Add the noodles and stir and toss just until heated through, about 1 minute longer. Serve immediately.

Serves 4–6

Green Beans with Garlic and Basil

1½ lb (750 g) tender green beans,
   trimmed if desired
2 tablespoons olive oil
1 clove garlic, minced
2 tablespoons finely chopped fresh basil
salt and pepper

Stir-frying parboiled green beans in olive oil gives the beans a rich golden color, and then mixing them with garlic and fresh basil brings out their inherent sweetness. For the best results, look for tender medium-sized beans. Serve with any simple grilled, roasted or braised main course.

*B*ring a large saucepan three-fourths full of water to a boil. Add the beans and boil until barely tender and still slightly resistant to the bite, 5–7 minutes. Drain, immerse the beans in cold water to stop the cooking and drain well again.

In a wok or frying pan over medium-high heat, warm the olive oil, swirling to coat the bottom and sides of the pan. When the oil is hot, add the beans and stir and toss every 15–20 seconds until they just begin to brown, about 3 minutes. Add the garlic and basil and stir and toss for 30 seconds longer.

Remove from the heat, add salt and pepper to taste and toss to combine. Taste and adjust the seasonings. Serve immediately.

Serves 4–6

Spinach with Garlic

1 tablespoon olive oil

2 bunches spinach, about ½ lb (250 g) each, carefully washed and thoroughly dried

2 cloves garlic, minced

salt and pepper

1 tablespoon freshly grated Parmesan cheese

A simple dish that goes nicely with roast or grilled chicken or grilled steaks. A dusting of freshly grated Parmesan cheese brings all the flavors together.

In a wok or frying pan over medium-high heat, warm the olive oil, swirling to coat the bottom and sides of the pan. When the oil is hot, add the spinach and stir and toss rapidly for about 1 minute. Cover and cook until wilted, about 2 minutes longer. Uncover and raise the heat to high to boil away any excess liquid.

Add the garlic and cook for 1 minute longer. Season to taste with salt and pepper.

Spoon into a warmed serving bowl, sprinkle with the Parmesan cheese and toss to mix. Serve immediately.

Serves 2

Mixed Vegetables with Soy Sauce and Chili Oil

¼ cup (2 fl oz/60 ml) peanut or
  vegetable oil
1 small head cauliflower, ½–¾ lb
  (250–375 g), separated into small
  florets
1 small bunch broccoli, ½–¾ lb
  (250–375 g), separated into small
  florets
½ lb (250 g) small button mushrooms,
  stems removed
½ red bell pepper (capsicum), seeded,
  deribbed and cut into long strips
all-purpose stir-fry sauce (recipe on
  page 12)
¼ cup (2 fl oz/60 ml) chicken stock,
  preferably Chinese style (recipe on
  page 13)
½ teaspoon chili oil (recipe on page 13)

*Simmering the vegetables in the chicken stock helps to cook
them evenly. If you cannot find button mushrooms, halve larger
mushrooms. For a less fiery dish, omit the chili oil. This is a
wonderful side dish to accompany grilled or roast lamb.*

In a wok or frying pan over high heat, warm the peanut
or vegetable oil, swirling to coat the bottom and sides of
the pan. When the oil is very hot but not quite smoking,
add the cauliflower and broccoli and stir and toss gently
every 15–20 seconds until barely beginning to soften,
4–5 minutes.

Add the mushrooms and bell pepper to the pan and stir
and toss over high heat every 15–20 seconds until the
mushrooms are just cooked, 2–3 minutes. Quickly stir the
stir-fry sauce and add to the pan along with the stock.
Bring to a simmer, cover and cook until the vegetables are
well flavored with the sauce and tender, about 2 minutes.

Uncover and add the chili oil. Stir and toss until all the
vegetables are well coated. Taste and adjust the seasonings.
Serve immediately.

Serves 4

Butternut Squash with Tomatoes and Leeks

1 butternut squash, about 2 lb (1 kg)

3 tablespoons olive oil

1 leek, including tender green tops, carefully washed and finely chopped

1 clove garlic, minced

2 cups (12 oz/375 g) well-drained peeled, seeded and diced tomatoes (fresh or canned)

¾ cup (6 fl oz/180 ml) chicken stock

½ teaspoon salt

¼ teaspoon white pepper

3 tablespoons finely chopped fresh basil

This is a wonderful vegetarian main course served with fried rice or crusty bread and a salad. It is also excellent as an accompaniment to grilled chicken or beef. If you like, top with extra shredded basil just before serving.

*H*alve the squash and scoop out the seeds and any fibers. Peel the squash and cut the pulp into ¼-inch (6-mm) dice.

In a wok or frying pan over medium-high heat, warm 2 tablespoons of the olive oil, swirling to coat the bottom and sides of the pan. When the oil is hot, add the squash and stir and toss every 15–20 seconds until lightly browned, 3–5 minutes. Transfer to a dish.

Add the remaining 1 tablespoon olive oil to the pan over medium-high heat, again swirling to coat the pan. When the oil is hot, add the leek and stir and toss every 15–20 seconds until softened, 2–3 minutes. Add the garlic, tomatoes and stock and simmer for 1 minute.

Return the squash to the pan and stir and toss all the ingredients together. Cover and cook over medium-high heat until the squash is tender when pierced with a fork, 7–10 minutes. Uncover and add the salt, white pepper and basil, stirring and tossing to combine.

Taste and adjust the seasonings. If any excess moisture remains, cook uncovered over medium-high heat until the liquid evaporates; this should take only a minute or so. Serve immediately.

Serves 4–6

Eggplant in Spicy Chili Sauce

Serve this spicy eggplant dish with your favorite Asian main course or with noodles with spicy peanut sauce (recipe on page 71) and fragrant rainbow vegetable platter (page 94). It is also excellent served at room temperature or chilled. If you want a spicier dish, add more chili paste to taste.

FOR THE CHILI SAUCE:

1 tablespoon chili paste with garlic

2 tablespoons dry sherry

2 tablespoons soy sauce

½ teaspoon sugar

2 teaspoons cider vinegar

½ cup (4 fl oz/125 ml) chicken stock, preferably Chinese style (*recipe on page 13*)

3 tablespoons peanut or vegetable oil

1 globe eggplant (aubergine), about 1 lb (500 g), or 4 Asian (slender) eggplants, unpeeled, cut into 1-inch (2.5-cm) chunks

3 cloves garlic, minced

2 tablespoons finely chopped, peeled fresh ginger

4 green (spring) onions, including tender green tops, finely chopped

salt

2 teaspoons Asian sesame oil

*I*n a small bowl, stir together the chili paste, sherry, soy sauce, sugar, vinegar and stock. Set aside.

In a wok or frying pan over high heat, warm the peanut or vegetable oil, swirling to coat the bottom and sides of the pan. When the oil is very hot but not quite smoking, add the eggplant and stir and toss every 15–20 seconds until lightly browned, 2–3 minutes. Add the garlic, ginger and green onions and stir and toss for 1 minute longer. Quickly stir the chili sauce and add to the pan. Stir and toss every 15–20 seconds until well coated, about 3 minutes. Reduce the heat, cover and simmer until the eggplant is tender, 10–12 minutes.

Uncover and season to taste with salt. Drizzle with the sesame oil and serve immediately.

Serves 4

Sweet-and-Sour Turnips and Carrots with Sesame Seeds

FOR THE GLAZE:

¾ cup (6 fl oz/175 ml) chicken stock, preferably Chinese style (recipe on page 13)

2 tablespoons natural rice vinegar

2 tablespoons sugar

1 tablespoon soy sauce

2 teaspoons sesame seeds

3 tablespoons peanut or vegetable oil

4 carrots, halved lengthwise and cut into ¾-inch (2-cm) chunks

4 turnips, peeled, quartered and cut into ¾-inch (2-cm) chunks

2 teaspoons cornstarch dissolved in 3 tablespoons water

¼ teaspoon salt

⅛ teaspoon coarsely ground pepper

1 tablespoon finely chopped fresh parsley

Simple winter vegetables are lightly blanketed in a savory glaze and then finished with a sprinkling of toasted sesame seeds. Excellent with lemon-orange chicken (recipe on page 38).

To make the glaze, combine the stock, vinegar, sugar and soy sauce in a small bowl. Set aside.

In a dry wok or frying pan over medium heat, toast the sesame seeds, stirring constantly, until lightly browned, about 1 minute. Transfer to a dish and set aside.

Add the oil to the pan over high heat, swirling to coat the bottom and sides of the pan. When the oil is very hot but not quite smoking, add the carrots and turnips and stir and toss every 15–20 seconds until the vegetables just begin to brown, 5–6 minutes. Be sure to distribute the vegetables evenly in the pan so they come into maximum contact with the heat and cook evenly.

Quickly stir the glaze mixture and add to the pan. Reduce the heat to low so that it simmers gently, cover and cook until the vegetables are just tender, 10–12 minutes. Uncover and raise the heat to high for 1 minute to reduce the pan juices. At the same time, stir and toss the vegetables to make sure they all come into contact with the liquid.

Quickly stir the cornstarch mixture and add it to the pan along with the salt and pepper. Simmer over high heat, tossing to coat the vegetables evenly, just until the sauce thickens, about 1 minute. Taste and adjust the seasonings.

Transfer to a warmed serving bowl and sprinkle with the parsley and toasted sesame seeds. Serve immediately.

Serves 4–6

Vegetable Soup with Chinese Egg Noodles

6 oz (185 g) fresh Chinese egg noodles

4 tablespoons (2 fl oz/60 ml) peanut or vegetable oil

8 small fresh shiitake mushrooms, stems removed and caps cut into strips ½ inch (12 mm) wide

½ small Chinese cabbage, cored and shredded

1 small carrot, peeled and cut into thin strips 2 inches (5 cm) long and ½ inch (12 mm) wide

½ bunch spinach, carefully washed, about 2 cups (4 oz/125 g) firmly packed leaves

2 cloves garlic, minced

2 oz (60 g) cooked ham, finely diced

6 cups (48 fl oz/1.5 l) Chinese-style chicken stock (recipe on page 13)

Serve this soup in individual bowls as an elegant starter. Or, for a more casual meal, once all the vegetables are cooked, return them to the pan and add the drained noodles and hot stock, then serve the soup directly from the pan. Dried shiitake (black) mushrooms can be used in place of fresh ones, but soak them in boiling water to cover for 20 minutes first.

*B*ring a large saucepan three-fourths full of water to a boil and add the noodles. Boil until barely tender, about 3 minutes, then drain and set in a bowl of warm water to cover.

In a wok or frying pan over high heat, warm 3 tablespoons of the oil, swirling to coat the bottom and sides. When the oil is very hot but not quite smoking, add the mushrooms, cabbage and carrot and stir and toss every 15–20 seconds until the cabbage just begins to wilt, 3–4 minutes. Transfer to a dish.

Add the remaining 1 tablespoon oil to the pan over high heat, again swirling to coat the pan. When the oil is very hot but not quite smoking, add the spinach, garlic and ham and stir and toss every 15–20 seconds just until the spinach wilts, about 2 minutes. Remove from the heat.

Pour the stock into a saucepan and bring to a boil. Meanwhile, dividing them equally, arrange all the vegetables attractively in 4 large soup bowls. Drain the noodles and top each mound of vegetables with one-fourth of the noodles, twisting each portion into a small "bird's nest." So as not to disturb the arrangement, slowly pour in the hot stock. Serve immediately.

Serves 4

Fragrant Rainbow Vegetable Platter

FOR THE SAUCE:

1 tablespoon natural rice vinegar

1 tablespoon mirin

1 teaspoon cornstarch

2 teaspoons soy sauce

1 green (spring) onion, including
   tender green tops, minced

2 tablespoons peanut or vegetable oil

½ lb (250 g) small fresh mushrooms,
   stems removed and caps halved

2 small zucchini (courgettes), cut into
   strips 2 inches (5 cm) long, ¾ inch
   (2 cm) wide and ½ inch (12 mm)
   thick

1 red bell pepper (capsicum), seeded,
   deribbed and cut into strips 2 inches
   (5 cm) long and ¾ inch (2 cm) wide

1 cup (6 oz/185 g) canned baby corn,
   rinsed, drained and halved lengthwise

A highly aromatic, mildly sweet-and-sour glaze coats a rainbow of vegetables in this dish. If the mushrooms are very small, leave them whole. For an all-vegetable meal, pair this with tofu-vegetable fried rice (recipe on page 77).

To make the sauce, combine the vinegar, mirin, cornstarch, soy sauce and green onion in a small bowl and stir to dissolve the cornstarch. Set aside.

In a wok or frying pan over high heat, warm the oil, swirling to coat the bottom and sides of the pan. When the oil is very hot but not quite smoking, add the mushrooms, zucchini and bell pepper and stir and toss every 15–20 seconds until the vegetables are tender-crisp, 3–4 minutes. Be sure to distribute the vegetables evenly in the pan so they come into maximum contact with the heat and cook evenly. Add the baby corn and stir and toss for 1 minute.

Quickly stir the reserved sauce, add to the pan and stir and toss until all the ingredients are heated through and the sauce thickens slightly, 1 minute longer. Taste and adjust the seasonings. Serve immediately.

Serves 4

Celery, Zucchini and Carrots with Red Onion

¼ cup (2 fl oz/60 ml) peanut or vegetable oil

1 small red (Spanish) onion, thinly sliced

3 carrots, peeled and cut into strips 2 inches (5 cm) long, ¾ inch (2 cm) wide and ¼ inch (6 mm) thick

3 celery stalks, cut into strips 2 inches (5 cm) long, ¾ inch (2 cm) wide and ¼ inch (6 mm) thick

3 small zucchini (courgettes), cut into strips 2 inches (5 cm) long, ¾ inch (2 cm) wide and ¼ inch (6 mm) thick

2 cloves garlic, minced

1 tablespoon soy sauce

⅛ teaspoon coarsely ground pepper

1 tablespoon finely chopped fresh cilantro (fresh coriander)

This is a versatile side dish that can be adapted to whatever vegetables are fresh and in season. Other types of summer squash can replace the zucchini, and green beans or jicama can stand in for the celery or carrots. Substitute fresh basil, parsley or chives for the cilantro.

*I*n a wok or frying pan over high heat, warm the oil, swirling to coat the bottom and sides of the pan. When the oil is very hot but not quite smoking, add the onion and stir and toss every 15–20 seconds until slightly softened, 2–3 minutes. Push the onion to the side of the pan, then add the carrots and celery and stir and toss every 15–20 seconds until the vegetables are tender-crisp, 2–3 minutes. Add the zucchini and garlic and stir and toss all the vegetables together until the zucchini is just tender, 2–3 minutes longer.

Add the soy sauce, pepper and cilantro to the pan and stir and toss just until the vegetables are well mixed with the ingredients.

Taste and adjust the seasonings. Serve immediately.

Serves 4

Swiss Chard with Feta Cheese

2 tablespoons pine nuts
2 tablespoons peanut or vegetable oil
2 shallots, finely chopped
2 bunches red or green Swiss chard,
　　about ½ lb (250 g) each, carefully
　　washed, stalks removed and leaves
　　torn into 2-inch (5-cm) pieces
¼ cup (1¼ oz/37 g) crumbled feta
　　cheese
salt and pepper

If you can't find Swiss chard, use fresh spinach. The feta cheese melts and adds a delightful savory-salty counterpoint to the chard. Serve with grilled lamb chops or chicken.

*I*n a dry wok or frying pan over medium heat, toast the pine nuts, stirring constantly until lightly browned, 1–2 minutes. Watch carefully so they do not burn. Transfer to a bowl and set aside.

In the same pan over medium-high heat, warm the oil, swirling to coat the bottom and sides of the pan. When the oil is hot, add the shallots and stir and toss every 10–15 seconds until they just begin to brown, 1–2 minutes. Add the Swiss chard, toss well to coat with the oil, cover and cook until wilted, about 2 minutes. Uncover and turn up the heat to high to boil away any excess liquid.

When the liquid has boiled away, add the feta cheese, cover and cook until the cheese just begins to melt, about 30 seconds longer. If more liquid is released, carefully drain the chard in a sieve, being careful not to drain away any of the cheese.

Spoon into a warmed serving bowl. Season to taste with salt and pepper and top with the toasted pine nuts. Serve immediately.

Serves 4

Cabbage and Carrots with Chili

2 tablespoons pine nuts

1 teaspoon chili paste with garlic

2 tablespoons soy sauce

¼ cup (2 fl oz/60 ml) dry sherry

salt and pepper

3 tablespoons peanut or vegetable oil

1 leek, including tender green tops, carefully washed and finely chopped

2 carrots, peeled and cut into thin strips 2 inches (5 cm) long and ¾ inch (2 cm) wide

½ red bell pepper (capsicum), seeded, deribbed and cut into thin strips 2 inches (5 cm) long and ¾ inch (2 cm) wide

1 head green cabbage, about 1 lb (500 g), cored and finely shredded

This Asian-style side dish is crunchy and colorful and makes an excellent accompaniment to roast chicken or beef.

In a dry wok or frying pan over medium heat, toast the pine nuts, stirring constantly, until lightly browned, 1–2 minutes. Watch carefully so they do not burn. Transfer to a bowl and set aside.

In a small bowl, stir together the chili paste, soy sauce, sherry and salt and pepper to taste. Set aside.

In the same pan over medium-high heat, warm the oil, swirling to coat the bottom and sides of the pan. When the oil is hot, add the leek and stir and toss every 15–20 seconds until slightly softened, about 2 minutes. Add the carrots and bell pepper and stir and toss every 15–20 seconds until beginning to soften, about 3 minutes longer. Add the cabbage and stir and toss every 15–20 seconds until just wilted, about 3 minutes.

Quickly stir the chili paste mixture, add to the pan and stir to combine. Bring to a boil over high heat and cook for 1 minute longer, stirring once or twice. Taste and adjust the seasonings. Stir in the toasted pine nuts, or transfer to a warmed serving dish and sprinkle with the pine nuts. Serve immediately.

Serves 4–6

Sesame Treasure Vegetables

1 tablespoon sesame seeds

2 tablespoons peanut or vegetable oil

1 red bell pepper (capsicum), seeded, deribbed and thinly sliced

1 yellow bell pepper (capsicum), seeded, deribbed and thinly sliced

¼ lb (125 g) snow peas (mangetouts)

all-purpose stir-fry sauce (recipe on page 12)

½ teaspoon sesame oil

This is a quick and colorful vegetable dish—just what you want when a simple accompaniment is all that's needed.

*I*n a dry wok or frying pan over medium heat, toast the sesame seeds, stirring constantly, until lightly browned, about 1 minute. Watch carefully so they do not burn. Transfer to a dish and set aside.

Add the peanut or vegetable oil to the pan over high heat, swirling to coat the bottom and sides of the pan. When the oil is very hot but not quite smoking, add the red and yellow peppers and stir and toss every 15–20 seconds until they just begin to wilt, 2–3 minutes. Add the snow peas and stir and toss for 1 minute.

Quickly stir the stir-fry sauce and add to the pan over high heat. Simmer, stirring and tossing occasionally, for 1 minute. Taste and adjust the seasonings.

Drizzle with the sesame oil and sprinkle with the toasted sesame seeds. Serve immediately.

Serves 2 or 3

Glossary

The following glossary defines terms specifically as they relate to stir-frying, including major and unusual ingredients and basic techniques.

ALMONDS, SLIVERED BLANCHED
Because of their mellow, sweet flavor and satisfying crunch, almonds are used often as an ingredient or garnish in stir-fries. Blanched (skinless) and slivered almonds are sold prepackaged in food stores.

AVOCADO
The finest-flavored variety of this popular vegetable-fruit is the Haas, which has a pearlike shape and a thick, bumpy, dark green skin. Ripe, ready-to-use avocados will yield slightly to fingertip pressure.

BASIL
Sweet, spicy herb popular in Italian and French cooking, particularly as a seasoning for tomatoes and tomato sauces.

BEANS, FERMENTED BLACK
Also frequently labeled salted black beans, this traditional Chinese seasoning—available in Asian markets—is made by fermenting cooked black-skinned soybeans with brine and a seasoning of **ginger**, orange peel or five-spice powder. Those made with ginger, listed on the package ingredients, are considered to have a finer flavor. Usually sold in plastic packages; once opened, store at room temperature in an airtight container.

BOK CHOY
Chinese variety of cabbage with elongated crisp white stalks and dark green leaves, with a refreshing, slightly peppery flavor.

BUTTERNUT SQUASH
A pale yellowish tan winter squash with yellow to orange flesh. Commonly about 8–12 inches (20–30 cm) long, with a broad bulblike base and a more slender neck.

CABBAGE, CHINESE
Asian variety of cabbage with long, mild-flavored, pale green to white, crisp leaves, packed in tight, elongated heads. Also known as napa cabbage or celery cabbage. Available in Asian markets and well-stocked food stores.

CHILI OIL
Popular seasoning of sesame, nut or vegetable oil in which hot chilies have been steeped. Available in Asian markets and the specialty-food section of most food stores.

CHILI PASTE WITH GARLIC
Powerful Asian seasoning combining crushed red chilies and puréed fresh garlic; used sparingly to add rich, fiery flavor to stir-fried dishes and as a condiment. Available in jars in Asian markets.

CHILI PEPPERS, DRIED RED
A wide variety of small, dried red chili pods—available in Asian or Latin American markets and well-stocked food stores—can be used whole to add subtle fire to stir-fried recipes. Guests should be warned not to bite into the colorful peppers.

CHILI PEPPERS, JALAPEÑO
Small, thick-fleshed, fiery chili, usually sold green, although red ripened specimens can sometimes be found.

CILANTRO
Green, leafy herb resembling flat-leaf (Italian) **parsley,** with a sharp, aromatic, somewhat astringent flavor. Popular in Asian and Latin American cuisines. Also called fresh coriander and commonly referred to as Chinese parsley.

CORN
Before use, fresh sweet corn must be stripped of its green outer husks, and the fine inner silky threads must be removed. If a recipe calls for removing the raw kernels from an ear of corn, hold the ear by its pointed end, steadying its stalk end on a cutting board. Using a sharp, sturdy knife, cut down and away from you along the ear, stripping off the kernels from the cob. Continue turning the ear with each cut.

CORN, BABY
Whole, entirely edible cobs of immature corn, no more than 2–3 inches (5–7.5 cm) long, are popular additions to Asian stir-fries. They are available canned in water in well-stocked food stores and Asian markets. Rinse well before using.

CORNSTARCH
Fine, powdery flour ground from the endosperm of corn—the white heart of the kernel—and used as a neutral-flavored thickening agent in stir-fry sauces, or to help form a crisp surface on stir-fried meat, chicken or seafood. Also known as cornflour.

BELL PEPPERS
Fresh, sweet-fleshed, bell-shaped member of the pepper family. Also known as capsicum. Most common in the unripe green form, although ripened red or yellow varieties are also available. Creamy pale yellow, orange and purple-black types can also be found.

To prepare a raw bell pepper, cut it in half lengthwise using a sharp knife. Pull out the stem section from each half, along with the cluster of seeds attached to it.

Remove any remaining seeds, along with any thin white membranes, or ribs, to which they are attached.

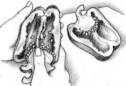

CUMIN

Middle Eastern spice with a strong, dusky, aromatic flavor, popular in cuisines of its region of origin along with those of Latin America, India and parts of Europe. Sold either ground or as whole, small, crescent-shaped seeds.

CURRY PASTE

Thick, powerful paste generally made from various spices, chili peppers, onions or **shallots** and garlic. Southeast Asian curry pastes also include fermented shrimp paste or **fish sauce.** Varieties of Thai curry paste include red, yellow and green, with the latter the hottest. Curry pastes are available in Asian markets and well-stocked food stores.

CURRY POWDER

Generic term for blends of spices commonly used to flavor East Indian–style dishes. Most curry powders will include coriander, **cumin**, chili powder, fenugreek and turmeric; other additions may include cardamom, cinnamon, cloves, allspice, fennel seeds and **ginger.**

EGGPLANTS

Vegetable-fruit, also known as aubergine, with tender, mildly earthy, sweet flesh. The shiny skins of eggplants vary in color from purple to red and from yellow to white, and their shapes range from small and oval to long and slender to large and pear shaped. The most common variety is large, purple and globular; but slender, purple Asian eggplants (below), more tender and with fewer, smaller seeds, are available with increasing frequency in food stores and vegetable markets.

EGGS, SEPARATING

To separate an egg, crack the shell in half by tapping it against the side of a bowl and then breaking it apart with your fingers. Holding the shell halves over the bowl, gently transfer the whole yolk back and forth between them, letting the clear white drop away into the bowl. Take care not to cut into the yolk with the edges of the shell. Transfer the yolk to another bowl.

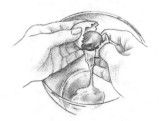

ESCAROLE

Variety of chicory with broad, bright green, refreshingly bitter leaves. Also known as Batavian endive.

FETA CHEESE

Crumbly textured Greek-style cheese made from goat's or sheep's milk, notable for its salty, slightly sharp flavor.

FISH SAUCE

Popular Southeast Asian seasoning prepared from salted, fermented fish, usually anchovies. Available in Asian markets and specialty-food sections of well-stocked food stores. Known variously as *nuoc mam* (Vietnamese), *nam pla* (Thai) and *patis* (Filipino).

GINGER

The rhizome of the tropical ginger plant, which yields a sweet, strong-flavored spice. Whole ginger rhizomes, commonly but mistakenly called roots, can be purchased fresh in a food store or vegetable market.

HOISIN SAUCE

Thick, reddish brown sauce of fermented soybeans or wheat, chilies, garlic, **vinegar,** sesame and Asian spices; used as a seasoning or sauce ingredient in stir-fries. Sold in bottles in Asian markets and well-stocked food stores, it keeps indefinitely in the refrigerator or cupboard.

LEEK

Sweet, moderately flavored member of the onion family, long and cylindrical in shape with a pale white root end and dark green leaves. Select firm, unblemished leeks, small to medium in size. Grown in sandy soil, the leafy-topped, multilayered vegetables require thorough cleaning:

Trim off the tough ends of the dark green leaves. Trim off the roots. If a recipe calls for leek whites only, trim off the dark green leaves where they meet the slender pale green part of the stem. Starting about 1 inch (2.5 cm) from the root end, slit the leek lengthwise.

Vigorously swish the leek in a basin or sink filled with cold water. Drain and rinse again; check to make sure that no dirt remains between the tightly packed pale portion of the leaves.

MIRIN

Sweetened Japanese rice wine used as a flavoring ingredient; available in Japanese markets and well-stocked food stores. Medium-dry **sherry** can be substituted.

MUSHROOMS

With their meaty textures and rich, earthy flavors, mushrooms are used to enrich many stir-fries. Cultivated white and brown mushrooms are widely available in food markets and greengrocers. Shiitakes, meaty-flavored Asian mushrooms, have flat, dark brown caps usually 2–3 inches (5–7.5 cm) in diameter and are available fresh with increasing frequency, particularly in Asian food shops. They are also sold dried, requiring soaking in boiling water to cover for approximately 20 minutes before use. In Chinese food markets, dried shiitakes are labeled black mushrooms. White, gray or pinkish oyster mushrooms, another popular Asian variety with lily-shaped caps, are sold fresh in Asian markets and well-stocked food stores. They have a tender texture and mild flavor faintly reminiscent of oysters.

Shiitake

Oyster

MUSTARD, DIJON

Dijon mustard is made in Dijon, France, from dark brown mustard seeds (unless otherwise marked *blanc*) and white wine or wine **vinegar.** Pale in color, fairly hot and sharp tasting, true Dijon mustard and non-French blends labeled Dijon style are widely available in food stores.

NOODLES

A wide selection of noodles, made from a variety of ingredients, are available in Asian markets for use in stir-fries. Wheat-flour noodles, fresh or dried and made with or without egg, are staples throughout Asia. They are usually labeled mein. Thin rice vermicelli and ribbon-shaped rice sticks, particular specialties of Southeast Asia, are made from pre-cooked rice. The vermicelli need no cooking—only soaking in water until soft; thicker rice sticks may require boiling until tender. Cellophane noodles—known by such other names as bean threads, silver noodles and transparent noodles—are made from mung bean starch in China and potato starch in Japan; cooked during manufacture, they generally require only soaking before use in recipes.

OILS

Oils not only conduct heat and prevent sticking during stir-frying, but can also subtly enhance the flavor of recipes in which they are used. Pale gold peanut oil is favored by many cooks for stir-frying because it can be heated to very high temperatures without smoking. It is also appreciated for its natural richness and subtle nutty flavor. Sesame oils from China and Japan are commonly made with roasted sesame seeds, resulting in a dark, strong oil used as a flavoring ingredient; their low smoking temperature makes them unsuitable for using alone for stir-frying. Olive oil is prized for its pure, fruity taste and golden to pale green hue. Relatively flavorless oils such as safflower, canola and other high-quality mild vegetable oils are used when no taste is desired from the oil.

Store all oils in airtight containers away from heat and light.

ONIONS

All manner of onions may be used to enhance the flavor, texture and color of stir-fries. Green onions (below), also called spring onions or scallions, are a variety harvested immature, leaves and all, before their bulbs have formed. The green and white parts may both be enjoyed, raw or cooked, for their mild but still pronounced onion flavor. Red (Spanish) onions are a mild, sweet variety of onion with purplish red skin and red-tinged white flesh. White-skinned, white-fleshed onions tend to be sweet and mild. Yellow onions are the common, white-fleshed, strong-flavored variety distinguished by their dry, yellowish brown skins.

PARSLEY

This popular fresh herb is available in two varieties: the more popular curly-leaf type and a flat-leaf type. The latter, also known as Italian parsley, has a more pronounced flavor and is preferred.

PEAS

Sweet garden peas, freshly shelled from their tough pods, are one of early summer's great delicacies; at other times of year, frozen peas—particularly the small variety labeled *petite peas*—are an acceptable substitute. Two related types of pea require no shelling, and are eaten pods and all. Snow peas, also known as Chinese pea pods or by the French *mangetout*—"eat it all"—are flat pods containing tiny, immature peas. Larger pods may require stringing before cooking. Plump sugar snap peas are a cross between garden peas and snow peas; some require stringing, while other varieties are stringless.

Sugar Snap Peas

Snow Peas

PESTO

Traditional Milanese sauce made of puréed **basil**, garlic, **pine nuts**, Parmesan cheese and olive oil; traditionally tossed with pasta and sometimes used as a seasoning for other dishes. Ready-made pesto can be found in the refrigerated section of well-stocked food stores.

PINE NUTS

Small, ivory-colored seeds extracted from the cones of a species of pine tree, with a rich, slightly resinous flavor. Used whole as an ingredient or garnish, or puréed as a thickener.

PLUM SAUCE

Sweet-tart Chinese bottled sauce of dried plums and apricots, sugar, **vinegar** and spices; used as a condiment. Available in Asian markets and well-stocked food stores.

PROSCIUTTO

Italian-style raw ham, a specialty of Parma, cured by dry-salting for 1 month, followed by air-drying in cool curing sheds for half a year or longer. Usually cut into tissue-thin slices, the better to appreciate its intense flavor and deep pink color.

RED PEPPER FLAKES

Coarsely ground flakes of dried red chilies, including seeds, which add moderately hot flavor to the foods they season.

RICE, LONG-GRAIN WHITE

Among the many varieties of rice grown, milled and cooked around the world, the most popular type is long-grain white rice, whose slender grains steam to a light, fluffy consistency.

SAKE

Although commonly thought of as Japanese rice wine, this aromatic, dry, clear, 30-proof liquid is actually brewed like beer. As with both wine and beer, it may be sipped with a meal or used as a cooking liquid.

SALSA, FRESH TOMATO

A cooked or raw Latin American sauce, most often one made from tomatoes, tomatillos or chilies. Fresh tomato-based salsa can be found in the refrigerated case of well-stocked food stores.

SCALLOPS

Bivalve mollusks that come in two common varieties: the round flesh of sea scallops is usually 1½ inches (4 cm) in diameter, while the bay scallop is considerably smaller. Usually sold already shelled.

SHALLOT
Small member of the onion family with brown skin, white-to-purple flesh and a flavor resembling a cross between sweet onion and garlic.

SHERRY, DRY
Fortified, cask-aged wine, ranging in varieties from dry to sweet, enjoyed as an aperitif and used as a flavoring in both savory and sweet recipes.

SOY SAUCE
Asian seasoning and condiment made from soybeans, wheat, salt and water. Seek out good-quality imported soy sauces; Chinese brands tend to be saltier than Japanese.

STOCK
Flavorful liquid derived from slowly simmering chicken, meat, fish or vegetables in water, along with herbs and aromatic vegetables. Used as the primary cooking liquid or moistening and flavoring agent in many recipes.

SWISS CHARD
Also known as chard or silverbeet, a leafy dark green vegetable with thick, crisp white or red stems and ribs. The green part, often trimmed from the stems and ribs, may be cooked like spinach and has a somewhat milder flavor.

TOFU
Also known as bean curd. Soft, custardlike curd, made from the milky liquid extracted from fresh soybeans, caused to solidify by a coagulating agent. Popular throughout Asia, fresh bean curd is widely available in Asian markets as well as in some food stores.

SHRIMP
Peeling and Deveining
Raw shrimp (prawns) are usually sold with the heads already removed but the shells still intact. Before cooking, they are often peeled and their thin, veinlike intestinal tracts removed.

Using your thumbs, split open the shrimp's thin shell along the concave side, between its two rows of legs. Peel away the shell.

Using a small, sharp knife, carefully make a shallow slit along the peeled shrimp's back, just deep enough to expose the long, usually dark, veinlike intestinal tract. With the tip of the knife or your fingers, lift up and pull out the vein, discarding it.

TOMATO
To peel fresh tomatoes, first bring a saucepan of water to a boil. Using a small, sharp knife, cut out the core from the stem end of the tomato. Then cut a shallow X in the skin at the tomato's base. Submerge for about 20 seconds in the boiling water, then remove and dip in a bowl of cold water.

Starting at the X, peel the skin from the tomato, using your fingertips and, if necessary, the knife blade.

To seed a tomato, cut it in half crosswise. Squeeze gently to force out the seed sacs.

VINEGARS
Literally "sour" wine, vinegar results when grape wine, apple cider, rice wine or other alcoholic liquid is allowed to ferment for a second time, turning it acidic. Natural rice vinegar is pale gold and has a slightly sweet, mild flavor. Look for rice vinegar in Asian markets and well-stocked food stores; avoid purchasing rice vinegar that has been preseasoned with sugar for use in sushi rice. Cider vinegar, made from apple cider, has a distinctive fruity aroma and flavor. Balsamic vinegar, a specialty of Modena, Italy, is a vinegar made from reduced grape juice and aged for many years.

WATER CHESTNUTS
Walnut-sized bulbs of an Asian plant grown in water, with brown skins concealing a refreshingly crisp, slightly sweet white flesh. Most often sold in cans already peeled and sometimes sliced or chopped, water chestnuts are occasionally found fresh in Asian food stores.

ZEST
Thin, brightly colored, outermost layer of a citrus fruit's peel, containing most of its aromatic essential oils—a lively source of flavor for stir-frying. Zest may be removed using one of two easy methods:
1. Use a simple tool known as a zester, drawing its sharp-edged holes across the fruit's skin to remove the zest in thin strips. Alternatively, use a fine hand-held grater.
2. Holding the edge of a paring knife or vegetable peeler away from you and almost parallel to the fruit's skin, carefully cut off the zest in thin strips, taking care not to remove any white pith with it. Then thinly slice or chop on a cutting board.

ZUCCHINI
Slender, tube-shaped relative of the squash, with edible green, yellow or green-and-cream-striped skin and pale, tender flesh. Also referred to as summer squash or courgette. Smaller squash have a finer texture and flavor, and less pronounced seeds, than larger ones.

Index

ACKNOWLEDGMENTS

The publishers would like to thank the following people and organizations for their generous assistance and support in producing this book:
Brigit Binns, Sharon C. Lott, Stephen W. Griswold, Ken DellaPenta, Jennifer Mullins, Jennifer Hauser, Tarji Mickelson, the buyers for Gardener's Eden, and the buyers and store managers for Hold Everything, Pottery Barn and Williams-Sonoma stores.

The following kindly lent props for the photography:
Biordi Art Imports, Candelier, Fillamento, Fredericksen Hardware, J. Goldsmith Antiques, Sue Fisher King, Lorraine Puckett, RH, and Chuck Williams.